Race and the Invisible Hand

G

THE GEORGE GUND FOUNDATION
IMPRINT IN AFRICAN AMERICAN STUDIES

The George Gund Foundation has endowed
this imprint to advance understanding of
the history, culture, and current issues
of African Americans.

Race and the Invisible Hand

*How White Networks Exclude Black Men
from Blue-Collar Jobs*

Deirdre A. Royster

UNIVERSITY OF CALIFORNIA PRESS

Berkeley   Los Angeles   London

*The publisher gratefully acknowledges the generous
contribution to this book provided by the African
American Studies Endowment Fund of the University
of California Press Associates, which is supported by
a major gift from the George Gund Foundation.*

University of California Press
Berkeley and Los Angeles, California

University of California Press, Ltd.
London, England

© 2003 by the Regents of the University of California

Library of Congress Cataloging-in-Publication Data

Royster, Deirdre A. (Deirde Alexia), 1966–.
    Race and the invisible hand : how white networks exclude
black men from blue-collar jobs / Deirdre A. Royster.
        p.   cm.
    Includes bibliographical references and index.
    ISBN 0–520–22999–1 (cloth : alk. paper) — ISBN 0–520–
23951–2 (pbk. : alk. paper)
    1. African Americans—Employment.   2. Discrimination
in employment—United States.   3. Blue collar workers—
United States.   I. Title.

HD8081.A65 R69   2003
331.13'3'0973—dc21   2002154103

Manufactured in the United States of America
12 11 10 09 08 07 06 05 04 03
10 9 8 7 6 5 4 3 2 1

For Dan Clawson and Deborah King
Twin pillars of strength in my intellectual journey

CONTENTS

TABLES

FOREWORD

For generations, even centuries, the advice dispensed to young black males has been, "Get a trade." This nugget of folk wisdom has also dominated scholarly discourse on race from Booker T. Washington to William Julius Wilson. In 1881, Washington founded the Tuskegee Institute, which provided instruction in such trades as carpentry, farming, and mechanics. A century later, Wilson traced the problems of the black lower class to a deficit of education and skills that, he assumed, accounted for the success of the black middle class. Between Washington and Wilson scores of social scientists, working with massive databases, have argued that black-white differentials in income largely reflected differences in occupational skills. The implicit message: Get a trade.

Race and the Invisible Hand is a study about young black males who heeded the conventional wisdom. They enrolled in a trade school in Baltimore, Maryland, whose mission was to prepare students for entry into respectable blue-collar trades. Glendale Vocational High School offered tutelage in such quintessentially blue-collar subjects as auto mechanics, electrical construction, industrial electronics, brick masonry, carpentry, printing, and drafting. It is true that in 1989–90, the years in which they graduated, Baltimore's economy was undergoing a major restructuring, and jobs in blue-collar trades were in short supply. But

Royster's main focus is on differences in outcome between black and white students. She determined this by assiduously tracking down graduates who remained in the Baltimore area and cobbling together a sample of fifty youth, whom she interviewed at length about their occupational trajectories from the day they marched proudly at graduation. Royster's skill as an interviewer is manifest in the heartrending stories she elicited from her subjects. One has to weep for these aspiring youth who "played by the rules," only to find themselves on the fringes of the labor market, unable to nail a job that would provide a modicum of dignity and allow them to support a family. However, "hard times" has an added racial dimension. Royster found that black graduates of Glendale Vocational High School were decidedly worse off than their white counterparts, and this provides the focal point of her study.

"Don't jump to conclusions." This is the refrain of leading scholars in the field who caution against invoking racism as the reason that blacks fare less well in the job market. Instead, they posit a gamut of other factors, all involving the putative deficiencies of blacks. It is alleged that young black men have an attitude. That they lack discipline and are unreliable as workers. That they are unwilling to do scut work. That they spurn jobs that pay low wages. That they lack the soft skills desired by employers. Etcetera, etcetera. Royster parries all these arguments by ingeniously tapping an unpublished study conducted under the direction of James Coleman in the 1960s, which buttresses her data for the 1990s. What do her data show? Compared to white students at Glendale Vocational High School, black students had better attendance rates and higher grades, they were less likely to have been in trouble with the police, they were willing to travel farther and to work for lower wages, and they were far less "choosy" about what jobs they would take. I don't want to steal any more of Royster's thunder. Suffice it to say that she provides an effective rebuttal to sociologists who claim that racism is ebbing and that the employment problems of lower-class blacks reflect their own deficits, whether of skills or culture. Her study forces us to confront anew the legacy of working-class racism, a structure that encompasses not only employers, workers, and labor unions, but also schools and teachers who, despite their best intentions, are implicated in the exclusion of blacks from coveted blue-collar jobs.

Race and the Invisible Hand is a dazzling example of how much can be achieved by a single enterprising researcher operating on a shoestring budget. Royster is a sociological David who, with a methodological slingshot, slays the Goliaths with their extravagant grants and massive databases. Of course, there will be critics who dismiss her study because it is not based on a "scientific sample," or because the findings of a case study cannot be safely generalized to the society at large. However, by leaving her cloistered environs at Johns Hopkins University, where she was a doctoral student, and venturing into some of Baltimore's poorest neighborhoods, Deirdre Royster has uncovered truths that shed new and different light on how the nation's working class was, and continues to be, a bastion of white privilege. *Race and the Invisible Hand* provides poignant and compelling testimony to the urgent importance of affirmative action, which, ironically enough, originated as a policy for countering entrenched racism in blue-collar trades.

Stephen Steinberg

ACKNOWLEDGMENTS

It is impossible for one with as poor a memory as mine to remember everyone who deserves thanks for helping to see this project to completion. Going back in time, I thank Mel Kohn, Alejandro Portes, William Julius Wilson, Patricia Fernandez-Kelly, Jomills Braddock, Darryll Parker, Judith Long, Rani Franovich, Trevor Rickford, Linda Pinkow, Sandy Johnson, Ben Feldman, Tony Austin, Lillian Thaniel, Martha Rawlings, Bharati Parekh, and my dad, Joseph Royster, who helped so much at the beginning of this journey. Of all those who believed in this project and supported it, none deserves more credit than Dan Clawson, without whose generosity the book simply would not have been written. I'm also thankful for Deborah King's readiness to listen to the chapters aloud and critique on short notice, as well as for her constant and gentle reminders that I was more important than the book. Robert Zussman and Margaret Cerullo read and commented on numerous drafts, made me believe in myself as a scholar, and held my hands through the process. My graduate students especially, but also my undergraduates, at the University of Massachusetts–Amherst provided endless encouragement and support — and I miss them. I am thankful to friends and colleagues at UMass-Amherst who stood by me through the process — Mary Deane Sorcinelli, Matthew Oulette, Deborah Koch, the late Andy

Anderson, Tracy Vaughn, Dee Weber, Jacqui Pinn, Dean Robinson, John Bracey, Louis Prisock, Enoch Page, Joya Misra, Agustin Lao-Montes, Sarah Babb, and my Lilly Fellows cohort. Stephen Steinberg, James Rosenbaum, Donald Tomaskovic-Devey, and Naomi Schneider read the manuscript and provided immensely helpful suggestions.

The research for this book was supported by a number of institutions. I am thankful for the support of the ASA Minority Fellowship Program, the National Science Foundation, the Social Science Research Council, the Center for the Social Organization of Schools at Johns Hopkins University, the Dartmouth College Thurgood Marshall Fellows Program, and the Social and Demographic Research Institute at the University of Massachusetts-Amherst.

Thanks also to my wonderful new colleagues and friends at the College of William and Mary and most especially to my partner, Michael Alan Lewis, who understands me and believes in closure.

My final thanks are to those who participated in my study, especially the fifty young men who shared their stories with me.

ONE

Introduction

Black researchers rarely, if ever, get to study white working-class people up close and personal, revealing their economic hopes, racial fears, and politically incorrect observations about the world. It simply isn't done. While white and black (as well as other) researchers regularly study the inner workings of poor and working-class communities of color, who seem to have become accustomed to being studied, typically only white researchers have been able to gain access to white poor and working-class enclaves. But if you want to understand how similar working-class blacks and whites assess and pursue opportunities, it is important to have face-to-face conversations with both groups. It is also important to create a comfort zone within which people can candidly discuss at least a few intimate details of their work and personal lives. This is easier said than done, particularly in the case of whites. Working-class, as well as more affluent, whites don't usually volunteer to share intimacies with researchers, and most black scholars choose (perhaps wisely) not to even try "going there." But, for reasons I'll explain shortly, I had to go there. I needed to understand first-hand how working-class whites dominate skilled blue-collar opportunities that make possible a modest but sound version of the good life without attending colleges, inheriting substantial family wealth, or hitting the lottery. I had to go there to see for myself what prevents many working-class blacks from being able to do the same.

In my case, going there meant venturing into segregated black and white spaces, each of which presented unique potential dangers. In cities of the early 1990s, even stable black neighborhoods were experiencing the horrible randomness of drive-by shootings, and in the white neighborhoods I entered, anti-black sentiments, like those voiced by the skinhead movement, were gaining prominence. Despite these issues — both of which seemed like mortal concerns before the research was underway — I knew I could do this work. Because I lived in one of the working-class black neighborhoods in which my black subjects lived (and was familiar with the others), I knew I wouldn't often get lost and felt that chances were low that I would find myself in serious danger as long as I used caution. I was extremely reluctant to enter neighborhoods in which there was known skinhead activity, but I chose to go there anyway. I could do so because I can pass for white.

Because I can pass for white, I have often overheard conversations among whites to which people of color are not ordinarily privy. At the same time, as a child growing up in an African American family and community, I observed differences — sometimes subtle — in conversation content when whites were present. I have lived as a proverbial "fly on the wall" observing the private talk of both whites and blacks — and my racially ambiguous appearance has made it possible to observe, if not always interpret, private race-talk among other racial and ethnic groups as well. I have observed a fascinating, and I would argue universal, pattern in my inadvertent eavesdropping sessions: Americans of all backgrounds talk about race even when they appear not to be talking about race and change their racially charged conversations when they believe members of other races are present.

This pattern of conversation management, with its intricate codes, euphemisms, and censoring, is connected to the desire of most Americans to appear colorblind, or racially neutral, particularly when they are observed by someone they consider a racial "other." This pattern makes it difficult for researchers who conduct cross-racial interviews to be certain that their informants are not adjusting their responses in order to seem as much like completely unprejudiced beings as possible — and it isn't a pattern that is observed only among whites. For respondents of color, the pattern can involve deemphasizing anger about racial conditions or concerns about being the victim of racial discrimination when speaking with white interviewers. For whites it may mean being careful not to espouse stereotypes about people of color when being interviewed by a researcher of color. Sometimes scholars as well as laypersons view with suspicion data collected in cross-racial interviews because we know about this pattern of self-censorship, even though we don't talk much about it. Experienced researchers frequently make arrangements for subjects to be interviewed by same-race interviewers, even when we don't expect the data to yield sensitive racial material, so concerned are we that race might contaminate the interview process. We can never be sure which characteristics in an interviewer might lead subjects to censor themselves, but we routinely place our cautionary bets on race rather than differences in education, social class, or even gender.

Because it was possible to signal to black subjects that I was a "sister struggling to get a degree from Hopkins" while presenting myself to whites as an ordinary (read white) graduate student with an atypical interest in and sympathy toward working-class folks, both the blacks and the whites that I interviewed seemed comfortable engaging in significant levels of private racial talk with me. Since I was a stranger, I am certain that members of both groups engaged in some censoring, particularly during the first fifteen to twenty minutes, but I am equally certain, given the candid material I collected, that most of my subjects shortly thereafter became very comfortable revealing private aspects of themselves. For example, a number of the white men I spoke with discussed their concern that affirmative action was helping less qualified blacks and hurting more qualified whites like themselves.

One young white man, Chip, felt confident that reverse discrimination had hurt his chances with the state police. He explained to me:

I applied for the state police and I passed all the tests and stuff like that. And we were down there for something, I forget what it was. And one of the [white] state troopers (we were on the side — a group of white male individuals), he said to us — [because] we obviously weren't selected to go further in pre-employment — he said, "I'm sorry fellas. Unfortunately, if you were black you would have had the job."

I asked Chip how that made him feel, and he continued:

It didn't make me feel any less of a person because I knew that I had the potential to get the job. I just feel that our system is a little bit screwed up the way sometimes . . . where it feels that it's obligated to certain minorities to give them a certain amount of jobs for each job. I feel — I'm working on the old system — you could get the job according to the qualifications. So I wouldn't expect to go down to a drafting company and have a guy who's got CAD [computer aided design] training and not get the job over me because I was black. As far as that goes, I feel there's a lot of discrimination against that [whites]. I feel you should be hired for your intelligence not your race.

Chip went on to tell me about how his buddies at the state police offices became angry about "reverse racism" after talking to the white state trooper and started complaining about the "fucking niggers" who had been awarded the jobs they wanted. Chip's comments — expressed uncensored — are eerily close to the more censored concerns I have observed among affluent whites during coded conversations about what factors produce persistent racial inequality. I have observed these codes most closely in my classes on race relations.

Year after year, my students at the University of Massachusetts–Amherst asked me — sometimes bluntly, as if to challenge, sometimes more discretely, as if we were discussing some deep personal secret not to be mentioned in public — why blacks have not yet caught up with whites in terms of economic achievements. I sensed that many of the students sincerely hoped that greater equality between blacks and whites in the United States was not far off. Others seemed to be expressing frustration with blacks for appearing to take longer than other groups to achieve the "American Dream." Still others seemed ambivalent about black progress—perhaps because they, like Chip, feared that black progress might mean fewer opportunities for whites like themselves.[1] This last group of students seemed the least satisfied with my lectures suggesting that historical forms of discrimination and exclusion do not die out simply because we have legislated against them.[2] Ironically, these same students were also likely to argue that "who you know" is frequently more important than "what you know" in the search for jobs. But somehow this logic—supported by research[3]—is never extended to African Americans, who, as a mere 13 percent of the population, are far less likely than members of the white majority to know the right people to get them the right jobs.

When I'd point out that blacks are still very much underrepresented in the more desirable occupations in the United States, these students countered that they knew whites who had lost a job, not been hired, or been passed over for a promotion that went to a black person for no reason other than race. It seemed that a narrow majority of my students felt that they or someone they knew had paid a price for the economic inclusion of black Americans that seemed both unfair and by and large regrettable.

Nearly all of my white students implied that we have reached a time when race shouldn't and doesn't matter, and, in those few places where it still does, it reflects the aberrant behavior of a few backward white people. Like Chip, they frequently suggested that when blacks lose in labor market competition with whites, it is solely because whites have superior qualifications. When blacks win, it is explained as the unfortunate result of a quota system that reserves positions for blacks, irrespective of qualifications.

Clearly, my students are not alone in their beliefs about labor competition between blacks and whites. Many whites outside of colleges and universities share similar views, including the notion that blacks are winning a disproportionate number of competitions because of government-sponsored affirmative action programs rather than merit.[4] White activists in California, for example, have mobilized around this suspicion in order to overturn affirmative action statutes affecting both educational slots and the process of awarding state contracts. Activists in twenty-five other states, including Texas, Washington, Michigan, Arizona, Colorado, and Florida, appear poised to follow suit.

While my students grant that historical patterns demonstrate that whites have been favored over blacks for four centuries, regardless of qualifications, they will not grant that such patterns have produced an unfair advantage held by whites as a group or a pattern of exclusion that the government has not adequately dismantled. Even when I ask students about jobs that don't require a college degree or highly specialized skills, like blue-collar trades, students authoritatively claim that blacks don't get these jobs because they do not work as hard as whites, they are less reliable than whites, and they have attitude problems that make them less desirable as workers, even on the rare occasions when they have the requisite skills.

From an economic point of view, my students' comments demonstrate a great faith in the "invisible hand." They assume that everyone who seeks work has an equal chance of being considered for jobs and that the best candidate is nearly always chosen irrespective of race or other irrelevant characteristics — *except when affirmative action interferes with this self-regulating system.* The "invisible hand" analogy suggests a sorting process that is free of particularistic bias and therefore inherently meritocratic. According to this worldview, anyone who studies and works hard ought to be able to make it in their chosen field. Faith in the "invisible hand" is associated with an endorsement of Market explanations of social inequality.[5] On the other hand, some of my students seem to endorse an alternative view, namely that many people get their jobs as a result of knowing the right people. Sociologists call this perspective the Embeddedness approach because it suggests that each person is embedded in a network of social relationships that help an individual accomplish a variety of goals, including getting a job. This approach brings to my mind the workings of a "visible hand" that interferes with the workings of the "invisible hand" and disrupts meritocratic sorting procedures. Not surprisingly, these two perspectives differ a great deal in how they explain the workings of complex labor markets that include young and minority job seekers, who are the main subject of this book.

A CRISIS IN THE YOUTH LABOR MARKET

Just as I started graduate school in Baltimore during the late 1980s, a number of journalists and researchers noticed a disturbing pattern of unemployment among young male workers, especially black men.[6] Young black men between the ages of 16 and 24 were over twice as likely to be unemployed as their white counterparts, and white men were having unprecedented employment problems.[7] In addition, growing numbers of black men were not even showing up in unemployment statistics because they had given up looking.[8] They were not in the labor force and they were not looking; scholars referred to them as discouraged workers. But this pattern was familiar to me long before I started graduate school.

Each year I was in college, I remember returning home for holidays and summer vacations only to find a number of my black male high school classmates and neighbors having puzzling difficulties finding and keeping jobs. I could not forget the sadness that seemed to envelop my friends, especially around the holidays, when everyone expects to shower family members with specially chosen gifts. Their inability to provide even small treasures for nieces and nephews caused many to withdraw from family life altogether — a self-imposed exile that no doubt made resisting alcohol, drugs, and other escape routes more difficult. By the time I started my second year of graduate school, three of my friends were dead, several others had spent time in jail, and numerous others — even those who "kept to the straight and narrow" — continued to have employment difficulties.

My observations led me to wonder if there was something about my friends, or something about the Washington, D.C., metropolitan area (where we grew up), or something about the late 1980s that caused these men to slip through the cracks. As a graduate student studying sociology, I was in a good position to begin a serious investigation. I found that sociologists, particularly those interested in understanding complex employment trends, frequently turn to large-scale studies that draw samples of individuals from all across the United States. National studies of non-college-bound males indicated that black men tended to take longer than white men to make the transition from high school to work; that they were paid less, on average, than comparable white men; and that they experienced greater pre– and post–high school unemployment than white men *and* black women.[9] Neither differences in men's work orientations — their attitudes about jobs and working — nor in their educational credentials accounted for these findings. My friends were not unique; their experiences were shared by many young black men across the United States.

The researchers who had been analyzing national data argued that the patterns most likely reflected contemporary racial discrimination and economic shifts that made fewer low-skilled jobs available to urban workers.[10] Others, consistent with the thinking of some of my students, suggested an alternative explanation: black men had poor attitudes and unrefined skills, not examined in the studies, that simply made them less desirable as workers than other available low-skilled groups.[11]

While national-level data provided important information about general trends, it could not address the concerns of those who felt that high school diplomas earned by blacks simply did not convey the competencies or the work-related attitudes that might be more readily assumed for whites.[12] Moreover, it wasn't clear whether black males were suffering in black/white labor market competitions because of discrimination or because of structural shifts in the economy that diminished the prospects of inner city residents (who were more likely to be black), while enhancing the prospects of suburban residents (who were more likely to be white).[13] National-level studies tended to concentrate mainly on outcomes rather than on the processes that led to diverse outcomes among young male job seekers. These types of concerns led some scholars to conduct new research that more closely examined how labor markets respond to black and white job seekers, paying critical attention to the educational experiences, attitudes, and other resources, including network assistance, that blacks and whites bring to the market.[14]

Researchers responded to the call for new studies with carefully designed experiments that trained black and white investigators to present themselves as job candidates in an identical fashion.[15] Researchers were trained to speak, dress, and respond to interviewers identically, while providing prospective employers with equivalent job applications, resumes that indicated identical educational accomplishments, and similar references and writing samples. In their study, Turner, Fix, and Struyk (1991) found that blacks were unable to advance in the hiring process as far as equivalent whites 20 percent of the time. They were denied a job offered to their white counterpart 15 percent of the time. This sort of study lent support to the idea that discrimination was a major factor hurting blacks in the labor market, even when black and white competitors held equally impressive records. But critics could easily point out that while such studies are disturbing, blacks and whites are not routinely trained to behave in exactly the same ways, nor are they likely to carry identical credentials and references in real job markets. Moreover, public concerns have been raised not about blacks who have impressive credentials, but rather about those who are, at best, high school graduates. In order to address these concerns, some researchers have suggested that, under ideal circumstances, researchers should compare individuals who had modest credentials and training from the same institutions and who competed in the same labor markets.[16] This is what I set out to do in my study. I quickly found out that, for blacks and whites, this is not as easy as it sounds.

Only in recent history have working-class blacks been able to compete relatively unimpeded in the same labor markets as whites, and despite the thirty years that have passed since the heyday of the Civil Rights era, it is still quite rare for blacks and whites to be trained side-by-side in the United States. Until the 1960s and 1970s, blacks and whites had little experience sharing access to the equalizing institutions in our society, most notably schools. While residential segregation, particularly in cities, has reverted to pre–Civil Rights era levels, mandatory school desegregation efforts have created only scattered pockets of multiracial school constituencies.[17] But these pockets are important social spaces, since they disrupt historical patterns of racial segregation and can encourage transracial networks of cooperation and collaboration. Researchers suggest that such spaces frequently become resegregated within the institution — as with ability grouping and tracking practices that place white and middle-income students in classrooms, floors, or buildings separate from their darker and poorer peers. In those cases, access to the same institution seems a nominal rather than instrumental similarity, and thus conceals important experiential differences.[18]

But surely there is some reason to hope that attending desegregated schools, particularly those in which blacks and whites share a track placement, could have the potential of disrupting all-too-familiar patterns of unequal achievement. I hoped to explore this potential by studying blacks and whites who attended the same vocational school and studied many of the same trades. For me, this was an important starting point, since I'd most likely be able to look at school records that would include information about attendance, behavioral problems, and grades, while examining relationships between schools and local employers, school personnel and students, and the young men and their friends and family members. I constructed my study to answer a set of basic questions:

What happens when whites and blacks share a track placement, the same teachers, and the same classrooms?

Can desegregated institutions, in this post–civil rights era, provide equal foundations and assistance for blacks and whites?

Does the problem of embeddedness — in this case, historically segregated job networks — stifle the emergence of cross-racial linkage mechanisms and networks beyond schools?

Or does the post–Civil Rights era provide a new, color-blind labor
    market in which blacks who show signs of work-readiness and
    achievement succeed on a par with white peers in terms of initial
    employment outcomes?

Finally, are black students, as the racial deficits theory suggests,
    lacking something that *should* make them less desirable as
    workers than their white peers?

These are the questions that guided me as I set about developing a
quasi-experimental research design that would replicate some of the useful characteristics of experiments while examining real people who were
searching for real jobs.

Between 1991 and 1994, I interviewed fifty men, equal numbers of
blacks and whites, who graduated in 1989 or 1990 from the Glendale
Vocational High School and who searched for entry-level jobs in
Baltimore's blue-collar labor market. By constructing a job history for
each, beginning with their first job and ending with their current or last
job, I was able to determine when and how the occupational trajectories
of the men began to diverge.

Although the majority of the whites and blacks performed well (all
were B or C students) and studied the same subjects — auto mechanics,
electrical construction, industrial electronics, brick masonry, carpentry,
printing, and drafting — whites experienced far greater success than
blacks. Specifically, whites held more jobs within their fields, earned
higher wages, experienced less unemployment, and had smoother transitions between jobs. They also got more effective assistance from family and friends and from white male teachers. Blacks, by contrast, often
relied on poorly situated black family members and friends, and received
only verbal encouragement, rather than material assistance, from white
male teachers.

Despite the advantages whites held over blacks — advantages not
linked to educational, motivational, or character differences — many
whites were convinced that blacks were unfairly advantaged because of

reverse discrimination. This ideology — fostered by whites who lived and socialized within racially segregated networks — served to create disincentives for including blacks and replaced the old black-inferiority rationale for exclusion with a new black-ascendancy rationale. According to this view, since the government was helping blacks but not whites, whites must help one another in the marketplace. None of the white males I spoke with had faced direct discrimination in the workplace, but a number held vague suspicions that they had lost out to blacks at some point or another. Only black males were able to provide specific examples of subtle and not-so-subtle forms of racism that they confronted in their dealings with white peers, teachers, employers, and customers. In numerous interviews, blacks described being forced to either adjust to poor treatment by whites or else face severely diminished job prospects.

This book provides an account of the school-to-work experiences of a set of young black and white men in the 1990s. Like many books that convey the results of a case study, the book is divided into sections that describe the thinking undergirding the study and its methodology as well as a number of its findings.

Chapter 2, "'Invisible' and Visible Hands: Racial Disparity in the Labor Market," provides a detailed examination of Market and Embeddedness explanations of racial inequality and labor-market sorting processes. Following the integrative framework introduced and advocated by Charles Tilly, in *Durable Inequality* (1998), the chapter draws on the work of numerous sociologists, economists, and historians. This chapter integrates the analytical frameworks of scholars who examine race, class, labor markets, and institutions (like schools), as well as processes, like going from school to work.

Chapter 3, "From School to Work . . . in Black and White: A Case Study," describes the school-to-work transition process in the United States and how my case study was designed to capture racial differences that I expected might emerge in the transition process. This chapter describes some of the difficulties of trying to conduct research on working-class, urban males, as well as the sometimes jarring experience of conducting "undercover" cross-racial research. I call my experience "undercover" because, as I mentioned earlier, I am routinely assumed to be white, but I am actually a very light-skinned African American. I confirmed that I had been taken for white through the explicit, rather than coded, racial talk in my interviews with white men and their families.

Chapter 4, "Getting a Job, Not Getting a Job: Employment Divergence Begins," describes the contemporary blue-collar labor market in cities like Baltimore and lays out a series of comparative findings on employment outcomes: wages, number and types of jobs held, on-the-job training acquired, months spent unemployed since graduating, and overall success patterns. Even though the case study sample consists of young men who are far better matched on relevant criteria than is possible in aggregate-level comparisons, the findings essentially replicate national statistics indicating that, on average, white men make faster transitions from school to work with more remunerative outcomes.

Chapter 5, "Evaluating Market Explanations: The Declining Significance of Race and Racial Deficits Approaches," uses unique data from this study and from an unpublished 1960s Baltimore study to evaluate the two most prominent Market explanations. The 1960s study, supervised by the late James Coleman, compared early labor market outcomes for white and black students who attended segregated vocational high schools in Baltimore, one of which later housed both the black and white students who were interviewed for the 1990s study. Comparisons of blacks and whites in both periods suggests the continuing and persistent, rather than declining, significance of racial barriers for blacks. The 1990s data also provide uniquely detailed comparisons of the white and black men on a variety of indicators, including attitude/behavior and skills, as well as willingness to work at dead-end jobs, reservation wage (the lowest wage that a respondent would accept), acceptable reasons to quit a job, school attendance, and troublesome behaviors, such as problems with teachers and illegal activities. The overwhelming similarities of these young men with regard to attitudes, behaviors, values, and grades — not to mention the uniformly polite and respectful demeanor I observed — strongly suggests that the employment differences that emerged during and after high school did not result from differences in these factors.

Chapter 6, "Embedded Transitions: School Ties and the Unanticipated Significance of Race," highlights the explanatory power of the Embeddedness framework and links the troubling employment findings to a set of social and institutional factors that made the process of choosing a vocational high school and the process of getting a job quite different for black and white men. Despite attending the same school, the black and white men received differential assistance from school personnel, especially from white male shop teachers, who offered verbal encouragement to black students while offering far more helpful material assistance to whites. Black males overwhelmingly relied on the formal transition mechanisms provided through the school, while white men combined highly effective informal school and personal resources. The school's part-time job placement counselor, a black woman, candidly discussed the racially charged employment setting that she observed through her role as the school-employer liaison. According to her, many local employers were former students of the school in its all-white days; many were still expecting work-study students to look like themselves. These patterns reinforced rigid racial customs that pervaded the homes and neighborhoods of the white men.

Chapter 7, "Networks of Inclusion, Networks of Exclusion: The Production and Maintenance of Segregated Opportunity Structures," provides an intimate examination of whites' taken-for-granted network advantages over similar blacks. Over and over again, white males mentioned this person or that person — friends, neighbors, family members, teachers — who continuously provided support and solid opportunities, even for those with poor work records or a history of incarceration. This chapter also examines black males' inability to tap into lucrative job networks, which made their searches increasingly difficult. Many were in the process of becoming the discouraged workers that we rarely read about and so often forget when we develop public policies. Even when black men were able to rely on friends for help, antiblack racism in the labor market had to be factored in strategically. This chapter captures lengthy conversations in the living and dining rooms of the young men and their families. Black men revealed painful experiences of racial discrimination, while white men, ironically, expressed outrage because many strongly believed significant opportunities were reserved for blacks. This chapter challenges the "a-racial" descriptions of job networks that permeate the economic sociology literature and suggests that reverse racism ideology is particularly dangerous, given the segregated social sphere within which it arises and is nurtured.

Chapter 8, "White Privilege and Black Accommodation: Where Past and Contemporary Discrimination Converge," discusses the explanatory power of Market and Embeddedness perspectives and advances three major conclusions that are in sync with Tilly's *Durable Inequality* thesis: (1) working class whites' monopoly over desirable working-class jobs has remained virtually unchanged since the Civil Rights era despite economic restructuring; (2) working-class/lower-middle-class black youth and their families have accommodated this reality by giving up, enduring pervasive racial discrimination, and developing costly alternative strategies without public policy assistance or significant political pressure from social justice organizations; and (3) customs linked to past discrimination have been maintained and refurbished ideologically by reverse racism propaganda, which makes supporting the inclusion of blacks tantamount to social suicide for young white men who are desperately dependent — socially and economically — upon older men in their networks. The price for attempting to break with the white-only tradition — ostracism and exclusion — would be unbearable, thus the torch of racial segregation is passed on from one generation to the next among the working-class white men I studied.

TWO

"Invisible" and Visible Hands

Racial Disparity in the Labor Market

Economists often speak of the problems of supply and demand when explaining the labor market difficulties of minorities and youth.[1] They explain that some workers experience unemployment when the demand for certain types of work(ers) goes down because of economic restructuring and cyclical downswings. This sort of cyclical unemployment is thought to last only as long as it takes such workers to find jobs in the growing sectors of the economy. Conversely, when the demand for certain types of work(ers) is high, but employers have difficulty finding an adequate supply of appropriate workers, unemployment and unfilled jobs in the economy are said to result from problems of labor supply. In addition to supply and demand problems, some employment difficulties result from " nonrational" behaviors among economic actors: for example, racial and gender discrimination by employers, or low-skilled workers rejecting available low-skilled jobs. Although such "non-rational" behaviors are often considered exceptions in an otherwise healthy free-market economy, the existence of supply-side and demand-side barriers that serve to undermine the unobstructed flow of persons into jobs is not disputed. Nevertheless, this system of supply and demand (if left unfettered) is thought to lead to relatively stable results that can be said to reflect a just equilibrium. With a few glitches here and there, equilibrium is accomplished through a relatively infallible "invisible hand" that sorts and selects workers within the free market. Based upon this logic, Market approaches to racial inequality explain labor market competitions that leave blacks in subordinate positions vis-à-vis whites as a function of differential abilities, differential demand for certain abilities, and/or differential ways of gauging what abilities a prospective employee has.

Sociologists who study economic action propose an alternative approach that focuses on how economic processes, going from school to work, for example, are embedded within interpersonal and institutional networks. The Embeddedness approach suggests that personal and institutional contacts may be extremely valuable in connecting workers to employment opportunities, and a lack of useful contacts may hinder many individuals — especially young and minority workers — from finding out about opportunities and being considered for available positions.[2] The Embeddedness approach then tends to analyze the processes and outcomes that leave blacks in less desirable positions vis-à-vis whites as a function of blacks not being historically or currently affiliated with well placed institutions or enmeshed in powerful informal networks where people share information and material assistance (actually hiring someone, for example).[3] Such opportunities, the Embeddedness approach suggests, provide the lubrication for getting things done — in short, they are necessary for learning about and preparing for opportunities, for gaining access to opportunities, and for being able to fully exploit opportunities once they have emerged.

Neither the Market nor the Embeddedness approach denies the overwhelming importance of racial segregation in determining racial disparity throughout most of U.S. history. Indeed, during the Civil Rights era, many economists and businessmen argued passionately that racial discrimination interfered with the proper functioning of markets by irrationally restricting both supply and demand. In other words, desirable black workers were prevented from finding and getting appropriate jobs, and employers were discouraged from fairly evaluating blacks who managed to become job candidates. Where the two approaches differ, however, is in the extent to which Civil Rights era struggles and subsequent legislation are seen to have eroded racially determined labor market processes that advantage whites while disadvantaging blacks.

The sort of racial inequality that emerges and crystallizes into permanent wage and employment gaps between equally deserving blacks and whites used to be easily explained. White racism, open and threatening, made it impossible for blacks to get and pursue their fair share of opportunities. As Americans have moved away from the early years of the civil rights struggle, explaining unequal racial outcomes has become more complex. While almost no one would argue that conventional white racism is completely gone, its heyday may be long past. Consequently, many are truly puzzled by the gaps that continue to emerge even among equally promising young whites and blacks. Others suggest that there is reason to be optimistic, since such gaps have grown smaller with time. Among those who endorse this market-oriented perspective, which implies that unearned white privilege has been effectively disrupted, none has been more prominent or persuasive than African American sociologist, William Julius Wilson.

WHITE PRIVILEGE DISRUPTED

In the late 1970s, Wilson published an extremely influential book, *The Declining Significance of Race*. In this book, Wilson argued that race was becoming less and less important in predicting the economic possibilities for well-educated African Americans. In other words, the black-led Civil Rights movement had been successful in removing many of the barriers that made it difficult, if not impossible, for well-trained blacks to gain access to appropriate educational and occupational opportunities. Wilson argued that this new pattern of much greater (but not perfect) access was unprecedented in the racial stratification system in the United States and that it would result in significant and lasting gains for African American families with significant educational attainment.

Recent research on the black middle class has only partially supported

Wilson's optimistic prognosis. While blacks did experience significant educational and occupational gains during the 1970s, their upward trajectory appears to have tapered off in the 1980s and 1990s. Moreover, some blacks have found themselves tracked into minority-oriented community relations positions within the professional and managerial occupational sphere. Even more troubling are data indicating that the proportion of blacks who attend and graduate from college appears to be shrinking, with the inevitable result that fewer blacks will have the credentials and skills necessary to get the better jobs in the growing technical and professional occupational categories. Despite real concerns about the stability of the black middle class and some glitches in the workings of the professional labor market, no one doubts that a substantial portion of the black population now enjoys access to middle-class opportunities and amenities — including decent homes, educational facilities, public services, and most importantly, jobs — commensurate with their substantial education and job experience, or in economic terms, their endowment of human capital.

While other scholars were investigating his theories about the black middle class, Wilson became distressed about the pessimistic prospects of blacks who were both poorly educated and increasingly isolated in urban ghettos with high rates of poverty and unemployment. His main concern was that changing labor demands that increase opportunities for highly skilled workers have the potential of making unskilled black labor obsolete. According to Wilson's next two books, *The Truly Disadvantaged* and *When Work Disappears*, this group's inability to gain access to mobility-enhancing educational opportunities is exacerbated by the further problems of a deficiency of useful employment contacts, lack of reliable transportation, crowded and substandard housing options, a growing sense of frustration, and an image among urban employers that blacks are undesirable workers, not to mention the loss of manufacturing and other blue-collar jobs. These factors, and a host of others, contribute to the extraordinarily difficult and unique problems faced by the poorest inner-city blacks in attempting to advance economically. Wilson and hundreds of other scholars — even those who disagree with certain aspects of his thesis — argue that this group needs special assistance in order to overcome the obstacles they face.

If Wilson intended the Declining Significance of Race thesis (and its Underclass corollary) to apply mainly to well educated blacks and ghetto residents, then Wilson only explained the life chances of at most 30 to 40 percent of the black population.[4] The rest of the black population neither resides in socially and geographically isolated ghettoes, nor holds significant human capital, in the form of college degrees or professional work experience. Looking at five-year cohorts beginning at the turn of the century, Mare found that the cohort born between 1946 and 1950 reached a record high when 13 percent of its members managed to earn bachelor's degrees. Recent cohorts born during the Civil Rights era (1960s) have not reached the 13 percent high mark set by the first cohort to benefit from Civil Rights era victories. As a result, today the total percentage of African Americans age 25 and over who have four or more years of college is just under 14 percent.[5] According to demographer Reynolds Farley, while college attendance rates for white males (age 18–24) have rebounded from dips in the 1970s back to about 40 percent, black male rates have remained constant at about 30 percent since the 1960s. Figures like these suggest that Civil Rights era "victories" have not resulted in increasing percentages of blacks gaining access to college training. Instead, most blacks today attempt to establish careers with only modest educational credentials, just as earlier cohorts did. Thus the vast majority of blacks are neither extremely poor nor particularly well educated; most blacks would be considered lower-middle- or working-class and modestly educated. That is, most blacks (75 percent) lack bachelor's degrees but hold high school diplomas or GEDs; most blacks (92 percent) are working rather than unemployed; and most (79 percent) work at jobs that are lower-white- or blue-collar rather than professional.[6] Given that modestly educated blacks make up the bulk of the black population, it is surprising that more attention has not been devoted to explicating the factors that influence their life chances.

Wilson's focus on the extremes within the black population, though understandable, points to a troubling underspecification in his thesis: it is unclear whether Wilson sees individuals with modest educational credentials — high school diplomas, GEDs, associate's degrees, or some college or other post-secondary training, but not the bachelor's degree — as cobeneficiaries of Civil Rights victories alongside more affluent blacks. The logic of his thesis implies that as long as they do not reside in socially and geographically isolated communities filled with poor and unemployed residents, from which industrial jobs have departed, then modestly educated blacks, like highly educated blacks, ought to do about as well as their white counterparts.

Because his thesis demonstrates considerable faith in the "invisible hand" (since laws have challenged discriminatory practices), Wilson's overall perspective should be seen as oriented to the Market approach rather than the Embeddedness approach, even though he acknowledges that one of the problems that black ghetto residents face is having few useful job contacts. Because he argues that *past* racial discrimination created the ghetto poor, or underclass, while macro-economic changes — and not current racial discrimination — explain their current economic plight, Wilson's perspective implies that white attempts to exclude blacks are probably of little significance today. In addition, Wilson offers a geographic, rather than racial, explanation for whites' labor market advantages when he argues that because most poor whites live outside urban centers, they do not suffer the same sort of structural dislocation or labor obsolescence as black ghetto residents. If Wilson's reasoning holds, there is no reason to expect parity among the poorest blacks and whites in the United States without significant government intervention. Despite a conspicuous silence regarding the prospects for parity among modestly educated blacks and whites, Wilson's corpus of research and theory offers the most race and class integrative Market approach available. First, Wilson specifies how supply and demand mechanisms work differently for blacks depending on their class status. Specifically, he argues that there is now a permanent and thriving pool (labor supply) of educationally competitive middle-class blacks, while simultaneously arguing that changes in the job structure in inner cities have disrupted the employment opportunities (labor demand) for poorer blacks. Second, Wilson argues that contemporary racial disparity results, by and large, from the structural difficulties faced by poor blacks rather than racial privileges enjoyed by (or racial discrimination practiced by) poor or more affluent whites. One of the questions guiding this study is whether the life chances of modestly educated whites and blacks are becoming more similar, as with blacks and whites who are well-educated, or more divergent, as with blacks and whites on the bottom.

ANOTHER MARKET APPROACH: THE RACIAL DEFICITS EXPLANATIONS

Within the Market approach, at least two other perspectives offer explanations for different employment outcomes among blacks and whites (with similar credentials) that differ significantly from those offered by Wilson. One explanation, associated with conservative scholars, suggests that blacks tend to exhibit fewer desirable cultural practices and values connected to work. The other explanation, associated with some economists and sociologists, emphasizes the importance of skills and achievement differences among blacks and whites that are either poorly measured or not included in statistical models that predict status attainment. The first approach assumes both skills and values deficits that make blacks less attractive to employers, while the second focuses more exclusively on the "inferior" skill sets of blacks. According to both perspectives, impartial employers simply reward the workers who bring the better skills and work values to the workplace — that is, the "invisible hand" does a fair job of sorting. Proponents of these positions agree with Wilson that earlier patterns that privileged whites at the expense of blacks have been disrupted, but they do not agree with Wilson that black joblessness results mainly from structural change. Rather, they argue that it results from racial deficits that simply make blacks the least desirable workers in the labor queue.

To reiterate, Wilson's structural-market emphasis suggests that one segment of blacks has skills assets that make them competitive, while another set — the poorest and most socially and geographically isolated blacks — have skills deficits that make them less desirable to employers. According to Wilson, such skills deficits, if operative, result from inadequate schooling, few chances to practice work skills, few contacts, and few role models. They are not, in Wilson's thinking, reflective of widespread black cultural patterns, but rather of the institutional collapse of the poor communities within which the poorest blacks live. Conservative scholars, such as Lawrence Mead, with whom Wilson has long argued, suggest that such skills deficits are joined with values deficits reflecting a cultural dysfunction that is more or less widespread among blacks. According to Mead:

> Although less than a third of blacks are poor in a given year, a majority of the long-term poor come from this group. Evidently, the worldview of blacks makes them uniquely prone to the attitudes contrary to work, and thus vulnerable to poverty and dependency.[7]

Conservative Dinesh D'Souza, echoes and amplifies Mead's themes:

> The main problem they [blacks] face in this country is not genetic deficiency, as alleged in the recent best-selling book *The Bell Curve: The Reshaping of American Life by Differences in Intelligence*, and it is not white racism, as asserted by many scholars and activists. Rather, it is that blacks have developed a culture that helped them to adapt in past circumstances but today is, in many respects, dysfunctional. . . . Contemporary African American culture is characterized by a high rate of illegitimate births, frequent resort to violence, and, among many of the young, scorn for hard work and academic achievement as forms of "acting white."[8]

Mead and D'Souza's arguments about the alleged cultural proclivities of blacks and their resultant economic difficulties hearkens back to ideas that were widely applied to white ethnic immigrants during much of the nineteenth century. Unfortunately, culturalistic Racial Deficits explanations have not yet been abandoned. Instead, they show considerable staying power and are increasingly the explanation of choice for racial inequality in both policy and layman's circles. There is a good reason why this so: it is a simple position, and one that has credibility as folk wisdom in American society.

American folk notions about group differences have always tended to elevate WASPs (white Anglo-Saxon protestants) over non-WASP groups. Even though the enormous labor needs of U.S. cities made places like New York and Boston much more friendly destinations than many labor-satiated European cities, ethnically distinct newcomers have always been viewed suspiciously by wealthier, ethnically homogenous white Americans.[9] These suspicions usually materialized as negative aspersions about a new group's presumed tendencies: "they" are lazier, less intelligent, less capable of controlling their emotions and appetites, less capable of governing themselves, and so forth. These folk notions were not merely harmless stereotypes, as both American Indians and Africans could attest, but in large measure determined the extent to which even white-skinned newcomers would be granted the rights and privileges associated with U.S. citizenship, as well as meaningful educational and economic opportunities. For example, some of the "common-sense" understandings that earlier arriving WASPs held about newcomers from Ireland, Poland, and Italy throughout the nineteenth century forced those groups to create ethnically insulated settlement strategies that reinforced the sense among outsiders that these groups were inordinately clannish. Not only were white ethnic immigrants expected to part ways with their coethnic communities and give up many of their cultural practices, but they were also expected to accept subordinate roles in U.S. society.

While numerous immigrants valiantly resisted pressures to accept subordinate roles and abandon cultural specificity, others took consolation that their plight as low-level industrial workers was not quite as unfortunate as the plight of blacks, who were, by and large, rural peasants during the latter part of the nineteenth century. Others came to appreciate dominance in the industrial sector as a privilege associated with white skin, and brutally oppressed the few blacks who managed to escape rural penury to compete for industrial opportunities.[10] It was as if the least fortunate white ethnic immigrants had decided, "By whatever means necessary, I will never be as unfortunate as blacks!"

Even as WASPs deemed most white ethnic immigrants unfit for anything other than manual labor, white ethnic immigrants, who frequently competed directly with free blacks for jobs and housing, came to voice antiblack ideologies that rivaled and surpassed the harsh pronouncements that were aimed at immigrants like themselves. Historian David Roediger suggests that these vulnerable white ethnic workers developed what could be called a "defensive racism" toward blacks that was in part a projection of their fears of not measuring up to both the requirements of industrial discipline and the reigning social morés of bourgeois WASP culture.[11]

Roediger provides persuasive evidence that these immigrants, many of whom had been forced to give up rural lifestyles as farmers, hunters, and shepherds, deeply resented industrial discipline and danger and, in their rhetoric, complained that the lives of rural black slaves were enviable in comparison. Roediger also suggests that this envy of and resentment toward blacks, free or enslaved, was manifested both in random and ruthless physical attacks against blacks and in hugely popular minstrel shows where whites in blackface portrayed "happy-go-lucky" slaves. Although working-class immigrants certainly resented oppression by more affluent native whites, resistance was limited, with the exception of labor organizing efforts, occasional rebellions, and efforts to disprove the reigning stereotypes. Stereotypes concerning the character, intelligence, and to a lesser extent, industrial skills of the white ethnic immigrants of this period closely resemble those that are now applied to black Americans, especially those residing in cities.

While it was once just "common sense" to see Italians as criminally inclined, Irish as chronic substance abusers, and Poles as intellectually handicapped, now it seems "common sense" to think of poor blacks and

Latinos as the latest of the losers. Unfortunately, stereotypes may be even more harmful now, since the jobs that sustained Italian, Irish, and Polish families, which mainly required stamina and brawn, are no longer in great supply. Now that language and computational skills are at a premium, not to mention the social skills seen as essential in retail and other service sector occupations, negative stereotypes about blacks' inability to do these jobs means black labor is unwanted.

But, putting aside cultural stereotypes, some argue that, unpleasant as it is to consider, there is more than a grain of truth to stereotypes about blacks' skill deficiencies. More sophisticated than the Culturalistic position, those who are concerned about race-based skills deficits suggest that there are hidden differences in the typical skill sets that similarly credentialed whites and blacks bring to the labor market. These skills differences, usually subsumed under the heading of cognitive skills, can be observed through achievement tests, grades, and other ostensibly objective measures. Such controversial concerns were raised during the late 1960s busing era, when sociologist Christopher Jencks and his numerous colleagues explained in their mammoth tome *Inequality* that unobserved or unmeasured variance in ability might be as likely to explain employment inequality as the more commonly presumed tendency among employers to discriminate against blacks.[12] More recently, similar concerns have arisen among economists and sociologists who are concerned that attributing inequality to discrimination rather than ability differences between blacks and whites diverts attention from the need for schools serving blacks and black parents to work harder to enhance black children's acquisition of human capital.

Economists Derek Neal and William Johnson clarify:

> Most studies do not adequately address the fact that, on average, blacks and whites enter the labor market with different levels of skill. Although years of school is typically used as a measure of worker skill, this variable is less than satisfactory. To begin, years of schooling is an inherently noisy measure of worker skill because it measures input, not an outcome. Moreover, years of school may system-

atically overstate the relative skill of blacks. . . . As a consequence, analyses that rely on schooling as a measure of skill will likely overstate the effect of current labor market discrimination on wages and confuse the barriers that black children face in acquiring human capital with the obstacles that black adults face when they enter the labor market.[13]

Sociologists Farkas and Vicknair echo these concerns and argue that differences in cognitive skills — specifically, word knowledge, paragraph comprehension, arithmetic reasoning, and mathematical knowledge — accounted for differences they found in black and white earnings, using data from the National Longitudinal Survey of Youth. Indeed, Farkas and Vicknair argued that including cognitive skills measures simply eliminated much of the unexplained variance in earnings that most scholars attribute to discrimination in the labor market.[14] Those who have critically examined these empirical efforts, such as Cancio, Evans, and Maume, point out that correlations between test scores and class background suggest that most of the observed differences between blacks and whites on standardized ability/achievement tests reflect class background factors rather than an independent effect of race.[15] Nevertheless, it is difficult to dismiss the argument that significant differences in the *quality* of educational credentials earned by white and black high school graduates (and thus different mastery levels) could account for unequal outcomes, especially since proponents of this position do not necessarily imply that blacks are generally intellectually inferior to whites, nor that black and white diploma holders are never functionally equivalent. Instead, these scholars typically argue that the schools attended by most whites are superior to the schools attended by most blacks; ergo, on average, white high school graduates have a qualitatively superior education — a more valuable diploma, if you will, than blacks. A variation on this theme suggests that having an equivalent number of years of education and even graduating from the same institution are crude measures of equivalence that could hide equally if not more important traits, such as grades, difficulty of courses taken and standardized test scores.

Because of the potential interference of class effects, Neal and Johnson suggest that ideally studies would compare blacks and whites who are as close as possible in premarket characteristics. They explain:

> Ideal data for estimating the effect of labor market discrimination on black-white wage gaps could be generated by a social experiment that observes a group of identically skilled teenagers both toward the end of secondary school and later during their labor market career. Everything relevant for wages that happens to them after secondary school could be affected by discrimination: post-secondary schooling, marriage, occupation, on-the-job learning, and so on. Under the assumption that there are no racial differences in discount rates or willingness to supply labor, the wage gaps observed during their careers would then represent the cumulative effects of labor market discrimination.[16]

I think Neal and Johnson are onto something here: it is important to compare the right sorts of people in order to properly investigate the influence of relevant premarket factors, employment discrimination, and other characteristics, like network assistance, which Neal and Johnson ignore, but which economic sociologists suggest may be extremely important.

CUMULATIVE WHITE PRIVILEGE: DURABLE RACIAL INEQUALITY

The Embeddedness approach suggests an alternative to both Racial Deficits approaches and Wilson's modified Market approach. This approach suggests that the employment difficulties of minority workers are the result of less efficacious personal, group-based, and institutional connections. From this perspective, for any given job, a number of candidates will probably have solid (or at least minimum) qualifications, but the person who is most likely to be alerted to the opportunity and selected will be the one who has the most efficacious personal, group-based, or institutional contacts, and not necessarily the most skilled person. That network structures — at the interpersonal, group, and institutional levels — are historically and contemporaneously affected by patterns of racial segregation in the United States makes determining whether networks traverse racial lines and whether they function in the same ways for members of different racial groups an important, if understudied, question for economic sociologists.[17]

Sociologists who study labor market processes, like getting a first job, have elaborated the concept of embeddedness as a feature of individuals, groups, and institutions. For example, according to sociologist Mark Granovetter, the job search is influenced not only by the number of contacts a person has but also by the strength of those interpersonal contacts. According to Granovetter, sometimes one's weak ties — mere acquaintances — help even more with job searches than those with whom one is quite close.[18] Since one's acquaintances are more likely to socialize beyond the spheres to which one is already privy, new and otherwise unavailable information and opportunities become accessible. Therefore, being *personally embedded* within a network that has many weak and strong ties can be particularly beneficial.

At the group level, network structures can become more complicated, as Alejandro Portes and Roger Waldinger have pointed out. Both sociologists have examined the overwhelming importance of immigrant networks in assisting newly arrived and long-term immigrant workers to find their way in urban economies like Miami and New York City.[19] Waldinger suggests that the networking efforts of ethnic immigrants have resulted in unique niche-penetration patterns among various racial and ethnic groups living in New York City, with the result that indigenous workers, like African Americans, have experienced a perpetual lock-out in some trades, like construction. Their sensitive examination of the exclusionary dimensions of ethnic networks has led these scholars to delineate what Portes and Landolt call the "downside of social capital" and what Waldinger refers to as the "other side of embeddedness."[20]

At the institutional level, sociologists James Rosenbaum, Mary Brinton and Takehiko Kariya, and Victor Nee, have pointed out the significance of people's ties to institutions.[21] In terms of work entry, the significance of institutional affiliations for individuals in the United States is far less well understood than in countries like Japan, Germany, and the United Kingdom. We also have very little information, at present, regarding the general ability of schools to connect workers to jobs/ employers or to supersede the sorts of informal patterns of exclusion that are frequently present in racially diverse societies. Nee points out that economists' concern with formal institutional arrangements, such as contracts, property rights, laws, regulations, and the state, have tended to downplay the potential importance of the ways in which informal norms and networks affect how institutions "act" economically.

The Embeddedness approach is particularly relevant to the class of blacks whose market dilemmas are least examined in existing research and theory, and which this book focuses on, namely, the black working class — those who are neither poor nor isolated enough to be considered underclass, nor well educated enough to be considered middle- or upper-class. The Embeddedness approach suggests that patterns of racial exclusion that were aimed at this class of blacks not only have continued to limit the life chances of contemporary cohorts, but have most likely had cumulative effects over time. For example, this perspective argues that white male workers continue to engage in customs of black exclusion which, in the 1930s, insured that only a few black men broke into the numerous semiskilled and skilled trade jobs that were then widely available. This early exclusion has cumulatively resulted in few older black men being able to pass on useful skills and use institutional (union) and personal ties to help younger black men survive the devastation of contemporary urban deindustrialization.

Because this approach is concerned with how individuals and institutions link or connect workers to jobs, it is *linkage* driven — as much as or perhaps more than supply-and-demand–driven. The Embeddedness approach tells a different story about labor market competition: a story in which visible hands, rather than an invisible hand, determine who gets hired. Historically, this story must begin with an examination of how white workers, males in particular, established early dominance in numerous urban labor markets and how exclusionary customs (exercised consciously and unconsciously) were not dismantled during the Civil Rights era, leading to what Tilly calls a pattern of durable inequality. Scholars in this tradition have focused mainly on the roles of white families, and to a lesser extent schools and employers, as informal occupational gatekeepers that allowed some blacks to earn a living but kept many from exploring their full potential as workers. In other words, the Embeddedness approach suggests that *visible hands* provide significant assistance to some but not all *and* not on the basis of formal criteria like skills and training. Tilly suggests that in order to understand patterns of durable racial inequality, we must examine the asymmetrical relationship of blacks and whites, looking specifically at how racially delineated economic *exploitation* allowed even less affluent whites to engage in *opportunity hoarding* behaviors and to *emulate* the exploitative and hoarding patterns of more affluent whites in institutions under their control, such as local markets, unions, and schools, in addition to *adapting* those same patterns as norms within interpersonal and community spheres. According to Tilly, "Exploitation and opportunity hoarding favor the installation of categorical (in this case race-based) inequality, while emulation and adaptation generalize (spread) its influence."[22] From this point of view, the earlier creation and contemporary maintenance of segregated networks and institutions does the work of perpetuating racial inequality by making everyday exclusionary behaviors a path of least resistance for contemporary whites.

BEYOND SKILLS AND TRAINING: THE ROLE OF SEGREGATED NETWORKS

Families and their networks of friends have always assisted young men and women in finding and getting jobs. Family members, family friends, and others within a network of extended contacts provide assistance to young workers in at least five important ways: (1) by sharing information about the operations of and particular openings within the labor market; (2) by employing them; (3) by recommending them for specific training programs or jobs; (4) by assisting them in learning specific job skills; and (5) by acting as mediators when difficulties arise in the work setting.

Certainly white families have held a historic advantage over black families in carrying out these functions.[23] In the past, even less educated white families were able, more often than most black families, to gain access to capital to finance small craft or trade enterprises where family members could be hired. Nonentrepreneurial white workers maintained an advantage by excluding blacks from unions, thereby preventing blacks from breaking into certain occupations or participating in intensive skills training programs, such as apprenticeships or internships. White working-class families, in addition to dominating formal and informal training opportunities, managed to regulate and monopolize entry into the better blue-collar occupations, and even entry into specific firms.

The best explanation for how some white workers managed to limit the opportunities of black workers is Edna Bonacich's Split Labor Market theory.[24] According to Bonacich, white male laborers engaged in riots throughout the nineteenth and early twentieth centuries against free blacks who occupied occupational niches that recent white arrivals coveted.[25] Until at least the 1960s, there were few sanctions against whites who attacked or even murdered blacks, so white workers were able to displace black laborers, craftsmen, and artisans through brute force throughout the nineteenth century and well into the twentieth. Because labor competition has always been embedded in this violent and multifaceted racial stratification system, which privileged whites of all classes, white workers were generally paid higher wages than blacks who performed the same work. White workers developed two strategies to preserve their race-based privileges in the labor market: exclusion and caste systems.

According to Bonacich, exclusion strategies involved preventing the physical presence of cheaper labor — especially nonwhite workers — in the employment area, thereby disrupting the system of supply and demand. Because nonwhite workers were prevented from participating in the labor pool and employers were frequently unable to undercut the position and wage rates of dominant white workers by hiring cheaper nonwhite workers, this strategy harmed nonwhite workers seeking access to jobs while protecting white workers, who were otherwise vulnerable to the cost-cutting strategies of employers. Historical research suggests that this pattern was rarely broken, and then only when blacks agitated and mobilized for inclusion first. The overwhelming pattern was one of attempts to exclude.

The imposition of a caste system was a less desirable but prominent option for white workers. Bonacich explains:

> If cheap labor is present in the market, and cannot be excluded, then higher paid labor will resort to a caste arrangement, which depends on exclusiveness rather than exclusion. Caste is essentially an aristocracy of labor, in which higher paid labor deals with the undercutting potential of cheaper labor by excluding them from certain types of work. The higher paid group controls certain jobs exclusively and gets paid at one scale of wages, while the cheaper group is restricted to another set of jobs and is paid at a lower scale. The labor market split is submerged because the differentially priced workers ideally never occupy the same position.[26]

Bonacich goes on to explain that caste systems tend to become "rigid and vigilant, developing a battery of laws, customs and beliefs aimed to prevent undercutting."[27] The imposition of caste systems involve at least three aims: (1) to monopolize, and in many cases privatize, the means of acquiring necessary trade skills; (2) to prevent the immediate use of cheaper labor as undercutters or strikebreakers in times of crisis; and (3) to weaken the cheaper labor group politically.

Examples of intimidation and violence against cheaper nonwhite laborers are abundant, but efforts to monopolize the acquisition of skills is a strategy that has been hidden in the practices of institutions such as schools and union apprentice programs, as suggested by Tilly's concept of emulation. For example, Briggs and Marshall's study of apprentice-ship in ten large cities in the early 1960s found that white-majority unions managed to prevent blacks from entering skilled trades and crafts by reserving slots for white workers — like legacy admissions practices that reserve college spaces for the children and grandchildren of the alumni of private colleges and universities.[28] In addition to recruiting only in all-white schools, the unions also used a number of clever exclu-sionary techniques: requiring applicants to take courses that were not offered in schools that served black students, to submit a recommenda-tion letter from a current union member, or to take entry exams if they had no union reference. These emulation strategies are especially clever because they appear to be neutral. That is, they don't appear to bar blacks; rather they rely on known information to create entry criteria that blacks are informally or structurally precluded from attaining.

Even though such strategies seem patently unfair and easily subject to challenge as civil rights violations, efforts by black tradesmen and others failed to dismantle the exclusionary practices of individuals, families, and unions, or those implicit in informal hiring practices in trades, such as construction. For example, in the 1980s, Mercer Sullivan found, in his comparative ethnography of young black, latino, and white males living in distressed urban communities, that the white males of Hamilton Park were able, thanks to well-placed friends and family members, to monop-olize the few desirable, high-paying, nonexportable jobs in the area, while the black males of Projectville and the latino males of La Barricada fell into spells of unemployment or into the unstable informal and ille-gal economies.[29] Waldinger and Bailey found in their study of employ-ment trends in the construction trades in New York City in the late 1980s that

> two factors, the importance of informal hiring and training practices
> and the political power of construction unions, have prevented
> blacks from achieving parity within the industry despite strenuous
> efforts to reach that goal.[30]

Waldinger and Bailey's findings highlight the importance of examining not only how relationships between families, unions, and local employers may help some workers — mainly whites — to become employed, but also how these same relationships serve as effective normative — or, to use Tilly's term, "adaptation" — barriers to work entry by other groups, such as black males.

Although black men and women have been at a disadvantage for some time vis-à-vis their white peers in helping young men with work entry, researchers think that the situation was exacerbated during the mid to late 1980s, when the pool of modestly educated individuals, especially men, who might have assisted with work entry was decimated through unemployment, underemployment, incarceration, and mortality rates that shocked the nation.[31] While both men and women became less efficacious contacts when they were forced to take contingent or temporary jobs, black incarceration rates and losses resulting from homicides made black men who were well positioned in the labor force pretty scarce. Persistent patterns of gender segregation and racial discrimination in the labor market have always resulted in black women's disproportionate placement in the least desirable jobs of the service sector and their exclusion from male-dominated skilled jobs, making them among the least effective contacts for gaining entry to the jobs young men would prefer to have.[32] Unfortunately for all workers, the dead-end jobs black women have usually occupied are among those increasing at the fastest rate in America's cities.

As the direct result of poor labor market prospects, many black men began opting for illegal wage-earning activities rather than the formal jobs generated in deindustrialized cities. Undoubtedly, many of these men have found illegal options more masculine, less demeaning, and more lucrative than the jobs held by their mothers, sisters, aunts, and girlfriends.[33] But to the particular disadvantage of these men, the country chose to get tough on crime just at this point and with a particular fervor attached to the illegal wage-earning activities in which black men were most likely to engage.[34] Not only have black men lost ground in the labor market, but political power has been effectively reduced as a result of the suspension of voting rights associated with felony convictions.[35] These political losses mean that black communities have effectively lost the ability to execute important political strategies. Specifically, now and in the immediate future, it would be extremely difficult (if not impossible) for blacks to create the sort of political machines utilized by white ethnic immigrants throughout the nineteenth and twentieth centuries to gain access to jobs, local/state/national influence, and social services. From the Embeddedness perspective, historical discrimination and contemporary discrimination have converged in the present. That is, continuing patterns of opportunity-hoarding among whites have exacerbated exploitative political and economic conditions that harm blacks. In this context, a focus on the presumed workings of "the invisible hand" subverts an examination of the observed workings of visible hands, with the result that even mild inclusive policies, such as affirmative action, are seen as disrupting purportedly fair sorting processes.

THREE

From School to Work . . . in Black and White

A Case Study

Occasionally scholars and policy makers come together to evaluate existing research and thinking on a compelling social problem. As youth unemployment (especially young black men's unemployment) was and is seen as an extremely compelling problem, several research teams and consortiums produced monographs in the 1980s and 1990s that described the problem in detail and evaluated much of the available research.[1] In their summaries, most of the reports pointed to gaps in existing research that made it difficult to determine what specific factors led to poor outcomes for black males. A number of the reports suggested that future research focus on the school-to-work transition process and utilize a variety of different research strategies, including the case study method, to fill in some of those gaps. In this chapter, I describe the case study method, what we know and don't know about the school-to-work transition for working-class black and white men, and how I designed my study.

WHY A CASE STUDY?

The case study — a systematic and in-depth investigation of one case — is a research strategy that is particularly useful for what researchers call "how" and "why" questions. "How" and "why" questions explore causal factors in processes or events that develop over time. When I began exploring the research literature on employment issues affecting working-class men, I found that existing studies that relied on survey and archival data had more than adequately answered "who," "what," "where," "how many," and "how much," but failed to get at some of the more puzzling "how" and "why" questions. Such studies did not adequately examine the combined influence of school personnel; students' grades, demeanor, or efforts to find work; personal connections; and local labor market conditions; thus it was impossible to evaluate the sorts of theoretical explanations I examined in Chapter 2. Indeed, it is still impossible to address a number of the reigning explanations of race-based labor market inequality using the data that is available through national surveys.

Another approach that some researchers pursued involved collecting new first-hand data from very small numbers of men. These ethnographic studies shed light on some of the "how" and "why" questions, but these studies failed to systematically examine relevant explanatory frameworks by comparing sufficient numbers of men on relevant factors. Richly descriptive explorations, such studies frequently focus on giving voice to small groups of urban males who are having the sort of difficulties that the national-level studies identify as endemic. Sometimes through participant observation, but more often through lengthy unstructured interviews, researchers — after gaining the subjects' trust — provided enormously useful information about the life experiences and worldviews of distressed urban men.[2] This sort of ethnographic research was and is extremely insightful, and even crucial in developing explanatory frameworks, but without systematic comparisons and information on factors beyond what subjects tell researchers, competing explanatory frameworks can only be partially evaluated. I was determined that there was a better strategy, which would enable me to better compare the value of the "invisible" and visible hands approaches.

According to case-study expert Robert Yin, when an analyst's objective is to juxtapose competing explanations of the same set of contemporary events, the case study is one of the most useful methodologies. In the case study, events cannot be manipulated as with an experiment, nor are events "dead" or unchanging, as with historical analysis; case studies more or less capture events as they are happening, and a holistic, real life/ real time, dynamic picture emerges without any manipulation by the researcher. Case studies usually differ from aggregate-level surveys and intimate ethnographic methodologies in their emphasis on studying processes. Nevertheless, researchers frequently combine some of the techniques of survey analysis and ethnography in their case-study methodology. By relying on semistructured interviewing techniques, for example, which use some of the same questions with all subjects but allow for considerable unstructured communication between researchers and subjects, the case study may build in some of the strengths of survey-based and ethnographic techniques.

Unfortunately, there are usually trade-offs associated with case studies, just as with other research methods. Because findings are based on one case — fixed geographically and in time, with one set of actors — results may not apply or be generalizable to a larger population. Settings, times, and actors may have idiosyncrasies that make a case unique. In addition, because in case studies researchers don't typically spend extensive time observing the day-to-day life patterns of subjects, important and relevant experiences may not be tapped. Researchers using the case-study approach are therefore obligated to explain to readers in what ways they attempted to minimize idiosyncrasies and to what extent they may have missed important aspects of subjects' experiences. I will address some of these issues later in this chapter.

GETTING A JOB THEN AND NOW

Until the last two decades, large numbers of young men living in industrial cities applied, during high school or after graduating, for jobs in heavy manufacturing, where salaries and benefits were relatively high, where job security was good. School counselors, like parents and students themselves, came to expect young men to follow the well-trodden path into heavy manufacturing or blue-collar jobs. Since so many fathers, brothers, and uncles worked as "blue-collar Joes," male students had little reason to believe that they would not be able to get similar jobs. At the time, stages of the school-work transition, at least for young work-bound men, often included some industrial training while in high school followed by a plant interview — usually arranged by a relative or family friend — a probationary period within the firm, and then, perhaps, a good word or sponsorship from someone who worked in the plant to close the deal. Employers at the time tended to look for young workers who had manual dexterity, were physically strong, and could be expected to be dependable. Many male students enrolled in vocational curriculums or schools to facilitate the work-entry process and avoid seemingly unnecessary academic courses.[3]

Since the late seventies, when manufacturing plants began to close in record numbers in the industrial cities, pathways from school to work — in manufacturing jobs — have decreased substantially. Consequently, school counselors, principals, and teachers sometimes find themselves having difficulty assisting work-bound students in finding desirable manufacturing jobs. Some counselors argue that, years ago, families took primary responsibility for assisting noncollege students with work-entry difficulties.[4] But now that many families no longer have access to jobs in manufacturing plants, schools are increasingly called upon to find ways to assist students in finding and getting work.

In the United States today, the role of schools in helping work-bound students to prepare for and make training or work transitions is not at all clear. Although many schools maintain institutionalized means for connecting college-bound students to colleges and universities, there does not appear to be a similar system for work-bound students who desire post–high school vocational training or skilled jobs.[5] It is possible that counselors and other school personnel act informally to prepare and link students with training or jobs, but little empirical research has been conducted to investigate how schools actually go about pursuing these tasks.[6] Unlike the college and university system, about which there is abundant information on application procedures, selection criteria, placement rates, and prestige ratings, we are just beginning to accumulate formal knowledge about special programs and opportunities for training- or work-bound students.

The contrast in how schools assist college-bound and work-bound students is stark. The early schooling, intermediate training, and occupational trajectories of college-bound students tend to flow in a carefully coordinated sequence, whereas noncollege-bound students typically find themselves searching for some pathway to skilled and semi-skilled jobs with little assistance from schools. Although nearly all students are, in principle, "bound for work," students who do not plan to go on to four-year colleges or universities, including students who plan to attend other postsecondary institutions, like junior colleges or trade and technical schools, are usually lumped together into the work-bound category.

College-bound or academically tracked students are expected to attend college after high school. Many institutional links and transition mechanisms exist to ensure that the needs of these students, in terms of postsecondary intermediate training options, are met. Guidance counselors can offer a great deal of advice regarding which colleges and universities will be likely to accept particular students and which are best able to help students secure appropriate jobs after graduating. Many counselors also know college recruiters personally and interact on a regular basis to link students to schools. Finally, high schools are often the setting for taking college entrance exams and meeting college recruiters and being interviewed. After college training, these students are expected to begin careers in professional and management occupations. Again, their transition from college to the professional world is assisted by coordinating mechanisms, in this case, between colleges and employers or graduate and professional schools. Their earnings, economic security, and standard of living tend to be high relative to those who did not attend college.

Students who are not placed on the academic track usually fall into one of several broadly defined subcategories, including vocational, general, and remedial track placements, and significant numbers of students become dropouts, either permanently or temporarily.[7] Students' initial track placements are very important, since the training and occupational trajectories that are possible with earlier track placement can vary considerably.[8] Usually students who were trained in vocational or technical schools or curricula are better prepared for semiskilled and skilled jobs than those who were placed in either the general or remedial tracks. In terms of student placement, black males tend to be disproportionately guided toward the lower general and remedial tracks, while white males are disproportionately steered toward academic tracks.[9] Consequently, the most comparable groups of black and white work-bound students are likely to be within a vocational track, where programs are designed to equip students with specific occupational skills.

The variety of intermediate training options that are available to work-bound youth after high school have never been systematically studied in the United States. Although local initiatives make an exhaustive listing impossible, some of the more common options include junior or community colleges, apprentice training and internships, established trade and technical schools, military training, miscellaneous accredited and nonaccredited training programs, and targeted public training programs. The jobs that are accessible to noncollege-educated adults tend to follow from their early curriculum track and work experiences or from their specialized intermediate training. For example, those trained in the most selective training programs are likely to get the skilled and semiskilled jobs — with fairly high wages and high levels of job security — while those who attempted to find work directly after graduating or who relied on nonaccredited training programs may find themselves able to get only entry-level jobs that provide little possibility for advancement. Many work-bound students skip intermediate training options and go directly into on-the-job training, which can lead to stable career-tracked jobs, depending on the firm. Others try out a few jobs, gain work experience, and settle into a permanent job long after their teenage years, when they have started families.[10] Still others join the military to get specialized job training and begin their careers.

If little is known about the variety of training or career options available to work-bound students in the United States, existing transition mechanisms designed to prepare students for and link students with training programs or jobs are similarly understudied. In several industrialized nations, there are extensive and explicit links between high schools and specific types of training programs, as well as specific employers. These countries see the effort to coordinate job training and work entry as a strategy that creates clear occupational paths, which in turn limits idle time between high school and work, when students who are not planning to go to college might engage in delinquent and other nonproductive activities. The German system, for example, is coordinated jointly by schools, employers, and training institutions, and is considered to be one of the best in the world at preparing noncollege-educated workers for complex industrial work. Consequently, training options such as apprenticeships can be as valuable and sought after as college training. In Germany, many high achievers in vocational curricula get choice apprentice assignments after high school.[11] In Japan, there are direct and enduring links between local schools and employers; each year employers send schools lists of jobs and skill requirements and request that top students be sent for interviews.[12] Consequently, Japanese counselors and teachers are sometimes able to use the incentive of rapid job placement to encourage high performance. Rosenbaum and others point out that the school-work transition systems designed in other nations were, ironically, modeled after the United States system for college-bound students.[13]

Although the importance of schools as preparatory and linking institutions for work-bound students in other nations is fairly clear, no existing studies enable us to determine whether schools in the United States play a consistent role throughout the country or even for a single, diverse student population. Examining the role of schools is particularly important in comparisons of black and white work-bound males, since studies that have used longitudinal data indicate that important differences emerge during the school-work transition.

Several researchers claim that, because the school-work transition in the United States tends to be uncoordinated and schools tend to lack stable institutional relationships with employers, most work-bound students tend to rely on friends and family, rather than schools, for help in finding training and jobs.[14] However, for minority youth, who are more likely than white youth to lack ties to employers, job-trainers, and other employed people in general, schools may provide the only available information about and connections to employers or other post high-school options. Failing to examine school-based connections would be to ignore a potentially equalizing resource, so one of my research goals was to find a school that trained both black and white students in blue-collar trades.

THE PROPOSED STUDY MEETS THE REAL WORLD

I have been told that even the most carefully designed study cannot anticipate the obstacles — perhaps more gingerly described as surprises — of the field or "real world" of the case study. Subjects do not show up on time or even keep appointments. Data promised from institutions does not arrive as promised, when promised, or how it was promised . . . or at all. Subjects refuse researchers access to relevant records. Interviews take place in dangerous or unfamiliar settings. In my study, I faced these and many other difficulties. And yet many of the obstacles that I encountered while conducting the research for this book provided invaluable insights into the difficulties of being young, working-class, male, and black (in half the cases) while at the same time seeking meaningful employment in a late industrial city.

The Location of the Study

In any case study, the first task is to either choose a site — a particular school, city, or organization, for example — or to evaluate a site that you are well-placed to use for practical reasons (a place where you already live, work, or have contacts). In my case, I chose to work in the city in which I was studying, Baltimore, Maryland. Although a study comparing the school-work transition patterns of white and black males could be conducted in a rural, suburban, or urban setting, I was lucky to be able to locate the study in a city because both the types of jobs — skilled crafts and trades — and the institutions (specifically, unions and established trade schools) that I am interested in are more likely to be located in cities. Baltimore turned out to be a solid location for my study because of at least three important criteria. Specifically, it had (1) a substantial population of both blacks and whites within the city; (2) occupational opportunities in both "good" jobs and jobs commonly considered "dead-end"[15]; and (3) political, social, and economic conditions that are not atypical among industrial cities in the United States.

Baltimore has more in common with the rust-belt, older industrial cities of the midwest and northeast — Detroit and Philadelphia, for example — than with the sun-belt cities of the south (Atlanta and Houston) or international tourist destination cities, like Los Angeles, New York, Miami, or San Francisco. But, like nearly all major American cities, Baltimore has undergone important social, economic, and political changes that have increased the number of black and poor residents. At the same time, Baltimore, like Chicago and Philadelphia, continues to house several majority-white working-class communities. I think Baltimore shares important characteristics with its peer cities in the midwest and northeast that increase the likelihood that findings in Baltimore can be generalized to those types of cities. For example, although Baltimore is smaller than many other industrialized cities and differs demographically by having extremely small numbers of Latino and Asian residents, it shares three important characteristics with other industrial cities. First, Baltimore is over 50 percent black. Second, over the last couple of decades Baltimore has experienced a loss in manufacturing and other blue-collar, male-dominated jobs, which may have led to the out-migration of a substantial number of white and black working-class families, who sought opportunities in surrounding suburbs. Third, Baltimore schools, like those of other major cities, are populated by a growing concentration of poor and minority students.

My second research task, in conducting a study that would take up where other studies have left off, was to identify a group of educationally comparable blacks and whites who were just entering Baltimore's labor market, that is, young men with very similar premarket characteristics. While only a few decades ago Baltimore had separate schools to serve its fairly large black and white populations, nearly every school that used to be majority white is now all or majority black. In the early 1960s, sociologists from Johns Hopkins University conducted a study that was designed to examine occupational and income inequality between blacks and whites in Baltimore.[16] Specifically, researchers asked: Do Negroes and whites in Baltimore with comparable education receive comparable jobs?" The researchers selected young men and women from nine graduating classes of Glendale and Wakefield Vocational-Technical High Schools in Baltimore. According to the researchers, "these two schools were proposed by the Equal Opportunity Commission as a strategic group to initiate a study of differential employment opportunities. Less than 2 percent of the students at [Glendale] are non-white; and none of the [Wakefield] students are white. Both high schools have comparable facilities and are staffed by teachers conforming to the same requirements."[17] Although both Glendale and Wakefield are still open and serving vocational students, the racial composition has changed drastically in Glendale, which is now over 50 percent black.

When the Johns Hopkins researchers compared students from Wakefield and Glendale, they hypothesized that "differences in the employment and earnings of students of the 2 schools would suggest differential treatment by employment agencies, unions or employers, or that the vocational guidance and placement programs warrant reappraisal."[18] However, because the schools were found to offer only a smattering of similar preparatory courses, researchers were unable to determine empirically whether inequalities resulted from access to different specialized training programs or from more systematic forms of racial exclusion. Given the increased diversity in the student population in Glendale, it is now possible, some thirty years after the project outlined above was conducted, to examine black and white students who attended the same high school and to take into account different coursework patterns and differential treatment by the same school personnel.

From the Baltimore City Public Schools, I obtained a master list of male students who were twelfth-graders at Glendale in 1989. Under ideal circumstances, I would have chosen four groups for my comparisons — black males, black females, white males, and white females — however, because of time and financial constraints, I chose to limit my study to males. This necessary limitation made sense given my hypotheses, which examined the importance of male-dominated institutions, such as trade unions, and outcomes in desirable jobs, which tend to be the province of males.

From the master list I had been given, I planned to randomly select fifty white and fifty black males. I then planned to interview the young men, the teachers they mentioned, and the employers they had interacted with over the course of their school-work transition.

Almost as soon as I received the list from the Baltimore Public Schools Office of Research, I realized that my task was far more complicated than I had anticipated. I first learned that it would be necessary to draw upon at least two cohorts of students to locate an adequate random sample. Thankfully, the Baltimore City Public Schools quickly provided me with a second list from the 1990 cohort. Then I learned that phone numbers and addresses collected from young men at the end of high school are almost completely obsolete within a two- to three-year period. I was able to interview fourteen white males that were selected randomly and another eleven who were identified by the first set of men — the snowball method of generating a sample — for a total of twenty-five. The lists I'd been given did not have accurate addresses or phone numbers for the eleven men I found with the help of their peers.

Although the black population from which I could select was larger than the white one, my efforts at creating a randomly selected population again failed. My research assistant and I checked the numbers and addresses of the black students on the lists. We found that only about half of the numbers and addresses could be accurate. With the list of possibly accurate numbers and addresses — those that were in service — of black students who had graduated in the 1989 or 1990 cohort, I randomly selected twenty-five students for the black sample. This method resulted in fifteen connections and, fortunately, all of the young men agreed to be interviewed. As with the white subjects, during the course of the interviews the black subjects assisted me in locating peers. Again, I was able to contact young men whose addresses and phone numbers had been inaccurate on the master lists. I managed to locate ten additional black men through this process, so that my total sample of black and white men was eventually fifty.

Help from the first sets of men I interviewed was key, since I found that young men seemed much more reluctant to turn down my request for an interview when I mentioned the classmate who had made it possible for me to contact them. I also felt more at ease going to the homes of men who first met me through their friends. I conducted most of the interviews in the homes of the young men over an eighteen-month period.

Even as I mourned the loss of randomization of subjects and the recognition that it would be possible to do only about half of the interviews that I had originally expected to do, I became engulfed in the rich detail of the stories told by each of the young men. Interviews that I had expected to take forty to sixty minutes began to take two to four hours — sometimes longer! Sometimes family members joined in to share their thoughts about the school-work transition or to mention an employment experience a son or brother had inadvertently left out. Inevitably, family members provided insights that were worth the minor disruption of my written questions, which though useful, only provided a context for the unique experiences of each young man.

I began with three major objectives: (1) to describe and compare stages of the transition process and general patterns for the two groups of young men; (2) to delineate the roles the young men and their families, schools, and employers played in structuring the school-work transition; and (3) to investigate the possibility that skills, values, and attitudinal differences might account for employment differences. To this end, I developed a data collection strategy that would allow me both to ask many specific questions about the young men's attitudes and experiences (such as reasons they felt were acceptable to quit a job, the number of jobs they had held, their wage histories, etc.) and to listen to their thoughts and feelings about how the school-work process was going and what factors were making a difference from their perspective and in their own words. I created a semistructured interview schedule using many questions from previous studies, and I recorded the young men's responses to my questions and their spontaneous observations on audiotapes.

I quickly observed that it was easiest to begin the conversation by charting the training and employment paths of the two groups of young men, starting with the eleventh or twelfth grade. I distinguished stages of the transition process for them, beginning with an examination of the pregraduation stage, during which they might have taken on work-study jobs or intensive training. Some might have used that time simply to frame in their minds their post–high school occupational aspirations. In my intensive interviews with the young men, I asked for the names of individuals, such as family members, and institutions, such as employment agencies or post–secondary schools, that were helpful or influential at the preemployment and active search stages. To examine institutional linkage mechanisms during the active search stage of transition, when students actually begin to approach employers, I asked the students to review their experiences carefully to determine if any mechanisms, formal or informal, existed or facilitated their work entry and how these mechanisms, if they existed, had been helpful. Finally, I asked the young men how well they had prepared for the labor market and how, with hindsight, they might interpret their first experiences.

I had planned to supplement information from the young men with information from employers whom they approached, but two dilemmas caused me not to seek contact with the young men's employers, former or current. Three of the first five white males that I interviewed asked that I not contact their employers for any reason. When I asked why, they replied that any questioning about them might draw attention to them in ways that could make them "suspect." When I asked in what way they might be suspect, they replied that anyone asking questions about them could draw suspicion, which made them uncomfortable. I reluctantly agreed not to contact their employers. Later, when I began interviewing young black men, I was surprised to find that many had either had no significant employment experiences yet or were unable to name the person who had hired them for the one or two mostly insignificant and short-term jobs they'd held. Among the black males with more stable school-work transitions, concerns resembling those of their white peers were mentioned. I chose not to contact any of the men's employers, even when they did not object, because I felt that their concerns could be justified.

I had hoped to gather information on how the young men's employers sorted and selected job applicants into "acceptable" and "unacceptable" categories, and how the outcome for each corresponded to the employer's stated selection criteria and process. Perhaps the real lesson I learned is that young men who are trying to establish themselves in a downsizing industrial economy are justifiably concerned about maintaining a noncontroversial relationship with employers past and present.

Of greater concern to me were the young men's responses regarding whether I could discuss them with their teachers at Glendale. Here there was a reversal of the employer scenario, with young black men expressing the greatest reservations about discussing them with their former teachers. Several of the black males felt uncomfortable about the possible responses of the teachers, suggesting, for example, that they doubted if the teacher would remember them. I had already spoken with a few of the teachers at the school, but I respected the students' wishes not to be discussed specifically. Four white males expressed a reluctance to participate in the study if I contacted employers or former teachers. Despite the students' reluctance to allow me to ask significant others about them, specifically teachers and employers, they volunteered a great deal of information about their experiences with specific employers and teachers. Oddly, many of the young men suggested peers who might have a different opinion of a teacher about whom a negative or positive impression was given.

The school placement counselor allowed me to interview her several times, despite a very busy schedule. Those interviews were the most helpful and significant of the twenty or so that I conducted with school personnel at Glendale. I kept coming back to the placement counselor because so many of the young men's experiences only made sense in light of the policies of the school regarding the rules of school-work transition. Ultimately the most important data for this study come from the young men, their school records, and the placement counselor.

I constructed short, ecological life histories for each young man, tracing his occupational trajectory from preemployment activities to employment outcomes. Because I collected retrospective data from the young men and supplemented their responses with secondary data from their high school records, I was able to create truncated life histories containing information on coursework, grades, attendance, post–high school training or job plans, and actual training and work activities during and after high school.

One concern was whether the timing of the study would allow a sufficient interval for differentiating patterns in the labor market experiences of white and black males. By the time of my interviews, these males had had more than two years to pursue jobs or training programs. Although one year is not usually enough time for male students to become stably employed, the interval was sufficient to evaluate their progress in getting into training programs or first jobs that might lead to stable careers. School counselors indicated that, by a year or two following graduation, most students who intended to pursue additional job training have either begun a specific program or given up the training strategy altogether. Counselors suggested that a one- or two-year fol-low-up interview would be an excellent time to compare white and black males, since students would have had at least eighteen months to pursue their training ambitions, and any differences in the transition patterns of blacks and whites would have emerged. They were correct, and each of my experiences in the field provided new insights into those differences.

AND WHAT ABOUT THE RESEARCHER?

In recent years, researchers have chosen to be more forthcoming about their perception of how some of their status characteristics — race, gen-der, age, and class, for example — may have affected the research process. In addition to revealing how such characteristics affect their choice of research questions and theoretical guides, researchers also speculate on how aspects of their person may affect how subjects respond to them. In essence, we attempt to estimate how revealing or secretive, honest or dishonest, comfortable or uncomfortable subjects were during interac-tions with us as researchers.

Because of these types of concerns, researchers sometimes suggest that we get the best information from subjects when they are comfort-able with us — that is, when our status characteristics and demeanor don't produce anxiety, fear, hostility, or other unwanted conditions that might make subjects less likely to give themselves over to the interview experience. Here is where being "good with people" and being known for "setting others at ease" can be an intangible but highly effective research strength. It could be argued that shared status characteristics facilitates the most open exchange between subjects and researchers; a similar logic applies when female detectives are selected to take the statements of rape victims.

Because my study involved interviewing young black and white work-ing-class men living in cities, at least two — but possibly many more — of my status characteristics might have affected the success of my interview strategies, namely, gender and race. Would young men reveal the truth about their labor market experiences — pay rates, firings, and so forth — to a woman whom they didn't know? Would some, finding me close in age, single, and (at least mildly) attractive, fudge their stories to sound as appealing as possible to me? Might I have an advantage, as a woman, since men might feel less comfortable revealing distressing labor market experiences to other men? To this day, I doubt that my gender adversely affected the interviews, although I should admit that I was asked on a few dates (by both black and white subjects), which I declined.

In Chapter 1, I alluded to the sadness I felt as my black male friends from high school found it difficult to become stably employed throughout the 1980s; their experiences were a major motivation for conducting this study. While I felt sympathetic to my friends and might have designed my case study around their lives, I knew talking to strangers would help me to be as objective as possible about the sources of black men's labor market difficulties. At the same time, I felt, given widespread deindustrialization, that it was entirely possible that white men might be having similar labor market difficulties, so just talking to black men would be insufficient.

Looking back, I recall excitement tinged with nervousness as I began calling up complete strangers for interviews. I remember hoping that a shared cultural background with the black men would help me to know how to put the "brothers" at ease, while I felt confident that my friendly and unassuming manner would help me to establish a rapport with both sets of men. I had one other "asset" that I knew could only help in making working-class white men feel at ease with me. Like a not insignificant number of African Americans in the United States, my physical appearance is virtually indistinguishable from European descent or "White" Americans. Most of my students, for example, guess that I am Italian, Jewish, Greek, or, on rarer occasions, Middle Eastern, Mexican, or "mixed," before learning of my African-American background in courses I teach on race and ethnicity. While I did not do or say anything to deny my African-American background in the interviews (and frequently used it to establish a quicker connection with my black subjects), nothing in my manner of speech, dress, or general appearance would have conveyed to my white subjects an African-American identity. It became absolutely clear that I was an undercover cross-racial researcher when the white men and some of their family members felt comfortable enough to criticize blacks in my presence, sometimes using epithets that made me sure I was "passing," even as I bristled inside with discomfort. Despite more than a few uncomfortable racial moments, I maintained my composure and (I believe) successfully hid my discomfort. At those times I would repeat a little mantra to myself: "I am a researcher getting facts from strangers who are generous enough to allow me into their homes and private lives — I can save challenging stereotypes and correcting inaccurate assumptions for my professors, peers, and the students who sit in my classes."

It isn't possible to fully anticipate the exigencies of entering the lives of strangers, however briefly, that come with conducting face-to-face interviews. My choice of subjects in some ways compounded my concerns about the appropriateness of my self-presentation and the possible difficulties I might encounter in unfamiliar settings. I was concerned about my style of dress, demeanor, and language, as well as whether to conduct the interviews in their familiar home settings or settings more familiar to me, like my office at Johns Hopkins, or in neutral places, like their work places or local parks or restaurants. I decided on an interview uniform that was more casual than formal. I wore a long, loose-fitting skirt, usually with a sweater or simple blouse, low-heeled leather boots, and modest make-up. I probably looked like I was in my mid to late twenties — which I was.

I decided against conducting the interviews at my home, though twice I found it prudent to break that rule. Instead, I went mainly to their homes (their first-choice locations) all over Baltimore and sometimes in outlying suburbs. I found that making the interviews convenient for them was a surefire way to get them to say yes rather than no. Several commented to me how odd they found it that I was willing to come to their homes to interview them; it seemed to be more impressive than the ten dollars that each one received to participate. I got the impression that my coming to them made them feel like I was some sort of journalist who might someday make them famous. I may have contributed to that belief by recording them on audiotape and relying on the interview schedule mainly as a tool for questioning rather than as a form I wished them to fill out. In any case, I am sure that most, if not all, of the young men were unaccustomed to being interviewed, and most expressed surprise at how rewarding the entire process was. I was able, perhaps because of an enthusiastic and interested demeanor and the mentioning of old classmates and notorious teachers, to get even the shyest of the subjects to spend at least an hour or two talking about life during and after Glendale. I feel that the respondents were extraordinarily candid, respectful, helpful, and thoughtful.

I scheduled nearly every white male for the morning or afternoon, usually on their days off from work. Since many men still lived at home, their mothers frequently helped make sure that their sons kept appointments with me, and some simply told me when to show up. I was comforted that some of the young men lived at home and that mothers would be expecting me, if not present during the interviews. I chose to conduct interviews with the white students first because I thought they might be a bit more difficult for me as an African American woman. I wasn't at all sure that I would "pass for white" during the interviews, although looking back, I realize now that there was no reason to think that I wouldn't. I was also concerned about class issues, since all subjects were informed that I was a graduate student from Johns Hopkins University. I didn't want anyone to feel uncomfortable about potential class differences or to worry that I might look down on them, so I worked hard to keep my language casual, direct, not too informal, but never stiff or haughty. I was never asked a direct or indirect question about my race, though I was often asked what it was like being a student at "Hopkins." In what I considered a moment for establishing some level of solidarity, I would answer that my own background had not prepared me for the elitism of an institution like Hopkins, but that I was doing my best to cope.

Several of the white males lived in areas that I knew to be strongly antiblack. Although those areas were not known for random violence, such as drive-by shootings, several had the reputation of having a burgeoning skinhead movement. I was extremely nervous whenever I had to go to those types of neighborhoods. Once I heard a large dog barking from inside a bald subject's house and I nearly fled. During the entire interview, I felt that the dog probably knew that I was masquerading as a white person and that I was really a black intruder. As I mentioned earlier, sometimes racially-biased comments made by the subjects or their family members infuriated me. During these times, it felt quite strange being in the houses of working-class whites who did not know my racial identification. Perhaps I would be remiss not to admit that, on those occasions, I felt a guilty pleasure in knowing that I was inadvertently fooling my white subjects. But, most of the time, the interviews were so inconspicuously pleasant and informative that any fears and dreads I may have had disappeared within minutes.

I had fewer reservations about interviewing young black men, but perhaps more reservations about going into their increasingly violent neighborhoods. Indeed, several of the black students were concerned enough for my safety to meet me at my car or to wait for me on their porch. For most of my life, I have had mostly pleasant interactions with young working-class black men. I also noticed when I made initial phone contact that young black men seemed more enthusiastic and less inconvenienced by the interview prospect. I detected a friendliness and lack of suspicion in many of the black subjects, and I tried to persuade the more reluctant men to give me the interview because I was a "sister struggling to get a degree from Hopkins" — no easy feat and certainly worth a sympathy point. I spoke playfully with the young men in an effort to let them know that I was not stuck up or inordinately enthralled by Hopkins, an institution that routinely elicited considerable antipathy from many of Baltimore's black as well as other less affluent families. I also felt comforted that a substantial number of my interviews with black males were to take place in black neighborhoods that were both familiar to me and considered relatively safe. I saved the scarier neighborhoods for last, usually making sure that someone would be able to accompany me. Without exception, the interviews went smoothly — though I had a few no-shows and sometimes felt awkward trying to hunt men down on beepers.

I hired a tall, black male research assistant to accompany me on evening interviews with black males, and I went alone on morning and afternoon interviews, as I did with white males. At one point, when interviews were scheduled nearly on top of each other, I trained Darryll, my research assistant, to conduct the interview — he had accompanied me to many, and he knew the routine. Sometimes mothers helped to set up the interviews, but more often the young men were home, so Darryll or I made the interview arrangements firsthand.

I told almost no one about the interviews taking place in the homes of potentially dangerous male strangers (white and black) and relied exclusively on a telephone safety routine that sometimes was pure acting on my part. The routine went something like this: I'd arrive at the home of a subject and ask to use the phone to connect with my research assistant, who I said might arrive sometime during the interview. I'd then call Darryll and chat for a minute or two, establishing some type of connection outside, mentioning who I was with, what time it was and the address and phone number of the subject, often providing directions as well. Sometimes I'd ask Darryll, in front of the subjects, if he'd located so-and-so to see if maybe the subject would volunteer help, and at other times I'd mention an interview that went great with so-and-so to try to gently pressure the respondent to enjoy and embrace the interview. I have no idea how my strategies affected the interview process, but I don't think they ever created harm. When Darryll wasn't home, I pretended to be talking to him or I called a friend.

I conducted forty-two of the fifty interviews (Darryll conducted the other eight) — all of the interviews with white subjects and most with the black subjects — without incident in neutral locations, like McDonalds and Patterson Park, in the young men's homes, and (in two instances) at my home. Each of these young men treated me with respect, patience, and kindness, several offering to walk me to my car after the interviews to insure my safety in some of Baltimore's more dangerous neighborhoods. My comfort level increased over the course of the study, as more and more of the young men would make calls to their friends telling them about the nature of the study and urging them to participate, or as I was able to mention an earlier interviewee in a contact call and find the tone of the potential interviewee's voice turn from indifference to mild enthusiasm.

SOME FINAL THOUGHTS ABOUT THE SAMPLE

The fifty young men interviewed for this study may have been, in some ways, atypical. For example, none of them had dropped out of school, and all were extremely polite and articulate. I suspect that these men were among the easiest to contact because of high residential stability and well-maintained friendship networks. Their phone numbers had remained the same or they had kept in touch with friends since graduating from high school two to three years earlier. Because of these factors, I may have tapped into a sample of men who were more likely to be success stories than most would have been. Researchers call this sampling dilemma creaming, because the sample may reflect those who were most likely to rise to the top or be seen as the cream of the crop, rather than those of average or mixed potential. In this study, however, it may have been an advantage to have "creamed," since I wanted to compare black and white men with as much potential for success as possible. Moreover, men who are personable and who have stable residences and friendship networks might be most able to tap into institutional and personal contacts in their job searches — one of my main research queries.

However, I'm not sure to what extent the sample should be viewed as special. More than half of the men I eventually contacted could not have been contacted had I relied solely on the formal lists provided by the Baltimore schools, so I have a mix of those who were residentially stable and those who simply stayed in contact with friends while moving around. In addition, while it is true that inner-city dropout rates are sometimes quite high at the national level, black high school graduation rates are comparable to white rates. Most young black men do hold high school diplomas (or GEDs) and, while many are stereotyped as inarticulate thugs with unstable home lives, I've never seen convincing evidence that this stereotype accurately represents more than a very small fraction of young black men, certainly not the majority, even among those who live in cities.

While I don't think there were idiosyncratic differences among the black and white men I studied or between the men I found and their same-race peers that I didn't find, some of the positive attributes of my sample suggest that my findings may generalize only to young men who generally play by the rules. Of course, it isn't all that clear what proportion of young working-class males (black or white) try to play by the rules — maybe the vast majority try to do so. Nor is it clear by what full set of criteria my subjects did, in fact, play by the rules. As later chapters will show, my sample includes men who had brushes with the law as well as some who might be considered "goody two-shoes." In other words, I'm not sure that the specific men with whom I spoke are atypical among working-class men, but I am willing to acknowledge that they may be. Perhaps what is most important to remember about the sample, who seemed to me to be pretty ordinary, "All-American" men, is my contention that this set of men *ought* to have similar levels of success in the blue-collar labor market — if, that is, we have finally reached a time when race doesn't matter.

FOUR

Getting a Job, Not Getting a Job

Employment Divergence Begins

If our society was colorblind — and groups such as African Americans were not disadvantaged as a result of racial preferences favoring whites — then young men like those I studied would experience the labor market quite similarly. That is, race would not help us to predict who did well or not so well in the labor market. This is not necessarily to say that young white men and young black men would have the same job outcomes, although having no differences would be very strong evidence indeed for a colorblind society. Rather, the possibility of a colorblind society rests on a more modest claim: that differences between whites and blacks can be explained by factors like skills, initiative, ability to work with others, and reliability. My research was designed to put that more modest claim to the test. The young men I studied — as I demonstrate in succeeding chapters — were selected precisely because conventional explanations for divergent outcomes do not apply to them. Both black and white students had attended the same school, performed at comparable levels, and demonstrated similar strengths and weaknesses of character. Nonetheless, even in this carefully matched sample, race continued to be a powerful predictor of wages and employment. In terms of wages, the median black man earned only 73 percent of the earnings of the median white man. In terms of unemployment, black men were 10 percent less likely than their white counterparts to be employed at the time of my interviews. This kind of employment divergence among equals suggests the need to carefully examine the underlying processes of going from school to work, and how such processes are affected by race. Before revealing the racially divergent transition patterns of the men in this study, it will be helpful to explore the types of jobs that are available today to young men.

GOOD JOBS, BAD JOBS: THEN AND NOW

Throughout the first half and much of the last half of the twentieth century, access to highly paid, skilled jobs in the central cities of the United States largely determined the economic stability of working-class families of both European and African ancestry.[1] Men without college degrees commonly worked as assemblers, packagers, fabricators, laborers, bricklayers, plumbers, carpenters, metal workers, electricians, longshoremen, welders, tile setters, machinists, installers, repairmen, groundskeepers, mechanics, printers, and tool and die makers. The list goes on and on. While the work was sometimes dirty, dangerous, and difficult, and not infrequently dull, a proliferation of trade unions helped over time to make work conditions safer and more remunerative. They also established rules of employment that significantly enhanced the desirability of these jobs. For example, in addition to reducing the typical workweek to five days and the twelve- to sixteen-hour workday to eight hours, many unions forced companies to tie workers' wages to productivity, eschew arbitrary promotion mechanisms, provide compensation for overtime work, insure workers against work-related injuries, and abide by seniority rules that protected older, more experienced workers from being displaced by cheaper, less experienced ones.[2] The income and other benefits from these jobs provided the least educated and least powerful men and women with the financial means to sponsor avenues of upward mobility for their children. The economic security and lifestyle that we think of as components of the "American

Dream"—including widespread home ownership, access to private transportation and other household amenities, savings accounts, retirement benefits, health and life insurance, and paid vacations—were made possible for large numbers of noncollege-educated workers principally through these blue-collar jobs and their unions.[3]

Since the late seventies, when manufacturing plants began to close in record numbers in the industrial cities, pathways from school to work in manufacturing jobs have narrowed substantially. Several hundred thousand jobs in manufacturing have either been eliminated or moved outside of central cities in the United States (Wilson, 1996). In Baltimore, where I conducted my study, over 70,000 manufacturing jobs were lost from the 1970s to the 1990s, when the men in my study were looking for work. Hardest hit was the heavy industrial sector, where jobs in metal industries, for example, went from 15,968 in 1970 to 2,463 in 1995. Jobs in nonelectrical machinery (construction, operation, and repair) went from 5,794 in 1970 to 1,316 in 1995. Even construction trades were halved in these decades. In 1970, Baltimore's economy supported 20,305 construction jobs; by 1995, that number had dropped to 10,226.[4] As a consequence, many young men have had difficulty finding any manufacturing or construction jobs, much less the desirable ones, which pay above the minimum wage, offer a career ladder, support health insurance coverage for workers and their families, and provide paid vacations.

Between the 1970s and 1990s, several industries that formerly provided numerous entry-level jobs in cities like Baltimore—auto, steel, shipping, and heavy manufacturing, just to mention a few—fell precipitously and are not expected to recover. Not all industries were hit this hard, but blue-collar trades like electrical and electronic equipment repairers, telephone installers and repairers, extractive occupations (mining), textile, apparel and furnishings machine operators, sewing and pressing machine operators, production inspectors, testers, samplers, and weighers all recorded losses between 1983 and 1996.[5] During the same period, a number of other blue-collar trades showed slight increases, including mechanics and repairers of automobiles and airplanes, data processing equipment repairers, carpenters and a few other construction trades, precision production occupations, machine operators, assemblers, inspectors, fabricators, hand-working occupations, transportation and material moving operations, handlers, equipment cleaners, and laborers. Overall, however, blue-collar jobs were not a growth area. In percentages, the blue-collar sector went from about 35 percent of the available jobs in the U.S. economy to about 15.4 percent in 1996.[6]

Increases occurred and continue to be expected, not in the blue-collar sectors to which many young men aspire, but rather in the service sectors, where less educated workers tend not to be unionized or particularly secure in the way blue-collar workers have been in the past. These changes are readily apparent in Baltimore: between 1970 and 1995, Baltimore's service sector increased from 79,957 jobs to 142,091.[7] It is hard to believe that in 1940 only 11.3 percent of U.S. jobs were in basic services, whereas in 1996 nearly 30 percent were.[8] Occupations not requiring college degrees with the largest expected job growth until 2005 are in basic service categories, including cashiers, janitors and cleaners, retail salespersons, waiters and waitresses, home health aids, guards, nursing aides, orderlies and attendants, child care workers, maintenance repairers (general utility), personal and home care aids, food preparation workers, hand packers and packagers, correction officers, amusement and recreation attendants, residential counselors, and general office clerks. Among the more traditional blue-collar occupations, only truck drivers and automotive mechanics are expected to rise as fast as these service sector occupations.[9]

For many young men, like the vocational graduates I studied, the bulk of the growing jobs in the service sector are less desirable for a number of reasons. First, they usually don't pay as well as blue-collar jobs. Entry-level wages in low-end service sector jobs usually start at the minimum wage and grow in very small increments over long time periods, whereas entry-level wages in the blue-collar sector typically start a few dollars above the minimum wage, with significant increases over time.[10] Second, few service sector jobs provide the crucial benefits packages — employer-provided health insurance, educational assistance, pension plans — associated with the blue-collar sector. Third, many employers seek temporary and part-time workers to fill service sector jobs, and young men typically prefer full-time, year-round employment.[11] Fourth, having trained for jobs in traditional male-dominated trades, many men resist female-dominated service sector occupations because they fear losing both their trade skills and their sense of masculine pride.[12] Consequently, young men who are now entering the labor force face greater competition for the remaining skilled jobs and are frequently forced to find alternative, less desirable occupations.

One way to get a sense of how different jobs are in the traditional blue-collar and growing service sectors is to examine the pre– and post–high school opportunities of one of the men I interviewed. Kurt, a highly successful white male student who majored in electronics, spent his high school years working in the service sector and his post-secondary years in the blue-collar sector. Like many young people, he'd worked part-time from the age of fourteen at a local restaurant, where he washed dishes and bussed tables starting at the minimum wage — at that time about $3.35/hour. Four years later, when he was about to graduate from high school, his job at the same restaurant paid $6.50/hour ($1.25 above an increased minimum wage). According to Kurt, the job was tedious, boring, and never offered any benefits. Older workers (mainly women) who had been there for years earned about the same wage as he did. He stayed for so long, he explained, because it was a local restaurant where he knew everyone, he could walk to work, he got free food, and he had friends who worked and ate there. Perhaps for these reasons, Kurt never tried to get a work-study job within his field during high school. By his senior year, he did apply (at the suggestion of two of his father's friends) for an apprenticeship with a local electricians' union. Shortly after graduating, he was accepted into the electricians' apprentice program, which started him off at $6.88/hour. Kurt was delighted to find that the apprenticeship also provided health and dental insurance, which made it possible for him to get off his parents' policies. Best of all, according to Kurt, were the apprentice-sponsored courses in electrical and math codes at a local community college — benefits Kurt says he would not have been able to afford on his own. Since starting the apprenticeship program, Kurt has been driving to work in his own car and acquiring valuable new skills in fields related to electrical construction, such as sheetrock application, welding, rigging, carpentry, and plumbing. His wages have risen steadily, in three-month intervals, since he started the apprenticeship. Not quite three years into the program, Kurt was earning $9.88/hour and expressed high hopes for his future, since more experienced electricians' helpers and journeymen were earning up to twice his hourly wage. The apprenticeship program provided an ideal transition mechanism for Kurt, since it guaranteed significant postsecondary educational and training opportunities, as well as job placement assurance.

For students who don't wind up in union-run apprentice programs, the school-work transition may take longer and not lead to the kinds of skilled jobs that are most desirable from the point of view of young men. A number of the men I interviewed had not been able, in the first three years after graduating, to move beyond the first jobs — almost always in the service sector — they started while in high school. Black men showed a troubling pattern of horizontal mobility in this regard, moving from one low-wage, low-prestige, service sector job to another without ever gaining a foothold in the blue-collar sphere.

In terms of good and bad jobs — those jobs that young men studying trades found desirable and those that nearly all considered dead-end — white males enjoyed an enormous advantage over black males. Table 1 indicates that most of the white males (19 out of 25) had already held at least one desirable blue-collar job in the first two to three years after graduating, while only 8 of 25 black men had done so. Even more telling, over half of the white men (15 out of 25) held a solid blue-collar job at the time of the interview, and slightly fewer (14) claimed that they had held more than one such job since eleventh grade. By contrast, only 5 black men in the study were employed in a good job at the time of my interviews, and only two had held more than one of these desirable jobs since eleventh grade. Black men's numbers were far greater in the bad job category, where, like their white peers, all had at one time or another held a low-paying, low-prestige service sector job. Unlike their white peers, however, 16 black men continued to hold such jobs, and 24 had held more than one such job since the eleventh grade. Only 8 white males remained in these undesirable jobs, and only 10 white males had ever held more than one such job.

Nearly half of the black men in this study had achieved very little success in the labor market; a substantial minority enjoyed moderate success. Moderately successful black men usually had not been able to get jobs in their field, but had been able to find a niche within the service sector that was acceptable, although not likely to lead to advancement. Most took a circuitous route, which involved a few less desirable service sector jobs and perhaps one significant blue-collar job, frequently in a field within which they had not trained. Gary's case is a good example.

Gary studied industrial electronics while at Glendale. During ninth and tenth grade, he worked as a fast food cashier, catching the bus to work and earning $3.75/hour. Like Kurt (and perhaps most young men), Gary kept this job primarily to earn spending change while in high school. When he was seventeen, he became a salesperson at Lockerplace (a sports attire and equipment store), where he earned $4.00/hour. Unable to find a job in his field of training, Gary capitalized on auto mechanics skills that he had honed informally. He left Lockerplace to take a work-study job with Foreign Motors, where he worked as a mechanic's helper for $4.00/hour for five months. Somewhat frustrated with the lack of opportunity in the city, Gary joined the army right after graduation, earning $600–700/month during his one-and-a-half-year stint in the service. After his military term, he returned to Baltimore looking for a job in auto mechanics. Instead of auto mechanics work, he was able to get a job at Mascot Distribution Services for $7.03/hour. Gary found this job in food services with the help of his mother and grandfather, who had also worked there. Because he lost his

Table 1. *Job Experiences of Respondents*

	White (N = 25)	Black (N = 25)
Had ever held a good job**	19	8
Currently held a good job**	15	5
Had held more than one good job***	14	2
Had received sponsored or on-the-job training***	9	0
Had ever held a bad job	25	25
Currently held a bad job*	8	16
Had held more than one bad job***	10	24
Had paid for additional postsecondary training**	7	17

Significance levels * <.05, ** <.01, *** <.001 based on two-sample tests of proportions.

car just before this job started, he often relied on his grandfather (who no longer worked there) or friends for transportation to and from the job. There were no buses to the worksite. This dependence was difficult, and Gary was forced to leave the Mascot job after five months. After a few months of unemployment, Gary began working at the two jobs he held at the time of the interview, one full- and one part-time. Gary combined full-time work as an auto mechanic at E. I. Pane for $7.25/hour with Saturday work at Lockerplace for $6.00/hour. Because he had no formal training in auto mechanics and couldn't afford to pursue any, Gary hoped that he could someday manage a Lockerplace store. He explained that he'd long ago given up his hopes for a job in industrial electronics.

Among black men who did not study traditional trades — choosing business studies or food preparation, for example — the growing service sector economy did not guarantee high levels of success. Tony's experiences provide a case in point. Tony majored in commercial foods while at Glendale. At sixteen, he got a work-study job at KD's Diner, where he worked part-time for $3.35/hour. Although it took Tony forty-five minutes to get to the job by bus, he stayed for a year. After high school, he was unemployed for two months, then took a job at Haldon (like K-mart) as a stockperson and cashier. He stayed for two years, beginning at $3.50/hour and ending at $4.25/hour. He quit to find a better job and within two weeks began working for Brun's Security as a guard. The job paid $6.00/hour, but Tony had to leave after two months because it took two hours to get to the job by bus and his parents would have been inconvenienced by having to take him to work daily. After another two weeks of unemployment, Tony began working in City National Bank's mail room, where he stayed for two months, working as a check processor for $4.50/hour. After yet another two-week spell of unemployment, Tony got a job at Aluminum Industries, which makes aluminum containers. Tony cannot remember what the Aluminum job paid, only that he got his current job while still working there. A friend of Tony's family doctor owned a local supermarket called Community Foods. Knowing that Tony was looking for work, Tony's doctor recommended him for a position at the Community Foods deli section. Tony had held the job for twenty months at the time of the interview; his duties included baking, cooking, general food preparation (meat, pasta, and vegetable salads), and food displays. He earned $5.70/hour and by the time of the interview had been able to purchase a car, which he drove to work (thirty minutes from home). Tony had been able to get a job in his chosen field, but his wage was less than one half that commanded by peers in blue-collar jobs.

A conspicuous difference between white and black men's early trajectories is the large number of black men (19) who attempted to increase their skill-sets and employability by paying for additional training themselves. While a few white men (7) attempted to pay for additional training, even more (9) had employers who paid for additional training. With a few exceptions, black men did not seek advanced certificates and training from trade schools, preferring instead to pursue associates' or bachelors' degrees from nearby historically black colleges. One rather sad exception was Jamal Hines, an industrial electronics student who sought security guard credentials after being laid off from his job driving a truck for a local produce company. Jamal had moved to the county with his wife and child, hoping to get a job as a security guard at a local drug store. After getting a student loan for $2,300 and faithfully attending classes at the Palser Security School, Jamal applied for a security job and was told by the interviewer that his credential from the Palser School was worthless because the school no longer existed. After making numerous calls, I discovered that there was no record of the company ever having existed. It had no certification record with local security standards commissions, and complaints had been filed against the (apparently defunct) company with the Maryland Better Business Bureau. Jamal was distraught by the time of the interview and was desperate to learn when his student loans were coming due. The pressure had taken its toll and Jamal seemed to be holding on by a thin thread, strengthened by his deep faith and an iron will not to disappoint his young family.

White men's experiences with postsecondary training were more fruitful. Several white men were pursuing technologically sophisticated training on the job or community college courses paid for by employers or apprentice programs. Among the highest paid, these young men were making rapid career progress, and most had exceeded minimum wage rates within the first year of employment, some earning twice that amount. It was exciting to learn about the ways that companies were investing in these young workers by sending them to specialized schools in fields like computer and auto repair, and how union-run apprenticeships were producing a new generation of journeymen. Some of these men began pursuing apprenticeships, apprentice-style training, or jobs in which employer-paid training was common while still in high school. In chapters 6 and 7, I examine the ways students become linked to these opportunities and why the white men seemed to gain access to these opportunities more often than the black men.

SUMMARY: SAD (BUT FAMILIAR) OVERALL
SUCCESS PATTERNS

One of my goals in this chapter was to provide an overall sense of how the black and white men's trajectories had begun to diverge only two to three years after high school graduation. While differences in the type of training that the men pursued and in the patterns of good and bad jobs indicated that black men could not expect to do as well as white men in the traditional trades, analysis of the overall patterns indicates the emergence at a very early career stage of a dire situation for the black men. One of the most disturbing trends that I detected in my analysis of overall patterns was the inability of black men to either successfully pursue the trades they had studied in high school or to recover successfully after switching trade preferences, as their white peers seemed to do easily. In this section, I describe overall success patterns, paying particular attention to the ability to remain in one's original field or to switch fields successfully, alongside more traditional criteria of success, such as wage rates, spells of unemployment, and employer-supported skill upgrades.

Whenever possible, I describe actual cases, but my main purpose is to set forth criteria and describe patterns that reflect success, as well as those that seem to reflect failure. In describing individual cases and sub-patterns, I highlight subtle but relevant details, like whether young men in the categories were likely to have acquired their own transportation and tools, whether some of their earnings might have come from informal (off-the-books) work, and whether they would have experienced long spells of unemployment. In this chapter, my main focus is describing the outcomes. In later chapters, I explore causal factors — in particular those that theorists claim contribute to different patterns of success and failure among black and white men.

Using data from the Glendale men as a guide, I identified two patterns of transition from school to work. In particular, I distinguish between those who found work within the field they prepared for while in school and those who have not built on that preparation. While the

pattern of transition is, as I will show, a matter of considerable importance, it does not, in itself, determine success. In each category, I found
men who were successful and unsuccessful, as measured by employment
and wages. In addition, a number of the men I studied were still in
school, and in effect had postponed the transition to work. If we examine the young men's experiences by success categories, I observed five
distinct categories: High Success Within Field (HSW); High Success
Outside Field (HSO); Moderate Success Within or Outside Field
(MSW/O); Low Success (LS); and Miscellaneous (MISC). While any
typology may be accused of arbitrariness, it does not seem unreasonable
to expect students' success to be related to their previous training within
a subfield; to be high, moderate, or low according to wages commanded
and other criteria; and to include a miscellaneous category for students
whose patterns are less identifiable along a traditional success contin-
uum. In the following sections, I provide more details about the criteria
that I used to identify the categories and provide examples within each.

High Success

Given that Glendale men are all vocational high school graduates, at
least some aspect of their success ought to be related to their progress
within the field they spent one to four years studying. Presumably,
young men who remained in their initial field of study would acquire
seniority before peers who switched fields somewhere in the transition
process. For this reason, I placed students who had held jobs, both formal and informal (off-the-books), within their initial fields and who have
managed to increase their wage rate over time to at least $7–8.00/hour
into the High Success Within Field (HSW) category. It is important to
recognize that some students could stumble into a pattern different from
the one they began in high school and ultimately become as successful
as those who stayed in their initial fields. It follows that such a pattern
would, at minimum, include a stable employment pattern with no or
very little unemployment, a wage of at least $7–8.00/hour, and a con-

sistent upgrade in skills within the new field. These men would be considered HSO, or High Success Outside Field. In both cases, it is not unusual for these men to have received substantial and valuable postsecondary training through their employers. One of the men mentioned earlier in this chapter, Kurt, exemplifies the high success pattern within field. One of Kurt's peers, Max, also experienced high success within his original trade field.

Max, a shy and sweet-natured young white man, had loved working on cars with his brothers, father, and uncles from an early age. Perhaps because being under the hood or chassis of a car required less social interaction than other fields, Max majored in auto mechanics while at Glendale. Like nearly all of the men in the study, Max's first job was working part-time for a local restaurant — in this case Benny's Seafood House. When Max was sixteen, his brother helped him snag a work-study job at U-Win Auto Rental. This job required Max to prepare cars to be cleaned, do some minor maintenance, and occasionally do oil changes. Max started out at minimum wage ($3.50/hour), but by the time he left after graduating, he was making $4.50/hour. Shortly after graduating, he got a job with Ash Putter Lincoln Mercury where, depending on what was needed, he worked as a lot man (moving cars around) or as a mechanic's assistant in the service department for $5.00/hour. After about nine months at Ash Putter, Max moved to Kendall Tires, to work as a tire changer, where he could earn substantial overtime at time-and-a-half. He advanced to mechanic's helper/technician I while at Kendall, but returned to Ash Putter after several months at Kendall. When he returned to Ash Putter, he was hired as a technician in a four-man team in the service department. With this promotion came significant wage increases, from $5.50 to $7.50 to $8.50 (his wage at the time of the interview). Max has been relatively happy with his latest job because he has plenty of opportunity to work overtime, and Ash Putter provides him with his own set of tools. Only back for one year, Max has taken several employer-sponsored courses in auto electric systems and specialized changing systems under Chrysler and Jeep/Eagle product maintenance shops.

While Max and Kurt represent young men who stayed the course with their initial training choices, some of the Glendale men were able to switch gears completely but land solidly on their feet — Jay is a case in point. Jay was a white machine shop major at Glendale who (in a now overwhelmingly familiar pattern) had worked as a busboy at LaFitte's from the ninth grade. In addition to working as a busboy during the school year, during summers Jay worked as a bar porter at the City Country Club. By the time he was sixteen, he'd managed to get a car, which he used to deliver pizzas, first for Peppi's, then Amore's and then Casa Mia's. Jay was delivering pizzas when he graduated and waiting to hear from the Baltimore Police Academy about his application to join the force. At one point while waiting on the Police Academy, Jay went with his dad to work at Arco Sheet Metal where he stayed for one week at $6–7.00/hour. He did not like working at Arco, so he quit and soon after got a job as a stockperson at Kids' City, which he kept for three months until he found out that he'd been accepted into the Police Academy. By the time of our interview, Jay had successfully completed his academy training and been on the beat for nearly a year. Jay makes $23,400.00 a year ($11.25/hour excluding benefits) and is very proud of the extensive benefit plan that comes with police work. His main duty is car-patrolling the all-black Melbourne Homes housing project in West Baltimore. Jay enjoys working as a police officer. He says that he knew other police officers before being accepted to the academy, but he refused to say whether any helped him get his current position. Jay is also pleased that he has an opportunity to study criminal justice at the City Community College through an employer-sponsored program. Even though Jay had (and passed up) at least one solid opportunity to work within his trade field, he has clearly landed a job that is more to his liking and that offers a similar (if not superior) salary and benefits package. For these reasons, he fits the High Success Outside Field pattern.

Very few black men met the criteria of high success either within or outside their chosen trade fields. One exception was Darnell, a black male student whose trade was not in a blue-collar field, but rather a

business field. Even so, Darnell's route to success has been far more circuitous than his white peers and remains unstable despite his considerable persistence. Darnell — a delightfully inquisitive young man — studied accounting while at Glendale, where he was a Commonwealth Plus
student (almost perfect attendance and above average grades). Between
the ages of fifteen and eighteen, Darnell worked at McDonalds, where he
earned $5.85/hour when he left. Clearly one of the most popular students
in school, he graduated from high school as the senior class president and
immediately took a job at Silvernet Bank in the accounting department
for $5.00/hour; his Glendale teachers had recommended him for the
position. After eight months, he took on a second job working at Anysort
Check Cashing, also for $5.00/hour. After two months of working at
both places, he chose the Anysort job, where after six months he was pro-
moted to assistant manager at $6.00/hour. Weeks later, he was trans-
ferred to Allsorts Check Cashing, where he was paid $13,800/year.
Darnell stayed for fourteen months at Allsorts, while taking classes in
accounting part-time at Murphy State University (a local, noncompeti-
tive four-year university). Darnell and his family were paying for his
classes at Murphy State because none of Darnell's employers had any
sort of educational reimbursement programs. Because he wished to focus more on school, Darnell left his full-time position at Allsorts to work
part-time at a neighborhood Hartingers. Darnell stayed at Hartingers
for about eight months, until he got a job as a youth counselor at the
Christopher Hackey School, where he supervises mentally challenged
male adolescents. At the time of our interview, Darnell was making
$18,500/year and said his benefits were modest (no educational assis-
tance, no dental plan, and a minimal health plan). He had been able to
purchase a car and drove twenty minutes to work each day. While he
continued to attend classes at Murphy State, Darnell was just beginning
to evaluate switching from accounting to human services, where he
thought public sector opportunities might be more abundant. I should
also mention Darnell's entrepreneurial project: he and three friends have
formed a business that specializes in arranging parties or party services

(such as disc jockeys) on the east coast. Though the company had not had any consistent success at the time of the interview (Darnell was unable to point to any earnings yet), he held high hopes for the company's future and his ability to contribute his accounting expertise.

While Darnell's ambivalence regarding his chosen field and his current job in human services differentiate him from his high-success white peers, most of Darnell's same-race peers would have been overjoyed to have matched his accomplishments. Instead, most have had moderate success since graduating from high school.

Moderate Success

A moderately successful path parallels the successful ones at a lower wage rate, since it may take place within or outside of the original field of study. I classified students as moderate success if there had been relatively stable but less consistent employment over time, with more or longer spells of unemployment than that experienced by the highly successful students. Additionally, the current job of the moderately successful would generally pay less than $8.00/hour, with most paying between $5.50 and $7.75 per hour. In these cases, students may have had some experience within their field, but their current job or the greatest number of their jobs were not in their original field. The stability of the career trajectories of these students did not appear as promising as the highly successful students. Nor did these men receive employer-sponsored training, though they sometimes obtained postsecondary training through their own or their family's initiative and sponsorship. Although a good number of black students occupy the moderate success category — Gary and Tony, mentioned earlier in this chapter, are examples — some white students also found themselves only moderately successful.

Chuck's experience provides a good example. Chuck studied drafting while at Glendale, but had a work-study job as a nursing assistant from the tenth through the twelfth grade. Chuck explained that his parents arranged for him to work at the nursing home where his grandparents lived, beginning at $4.35/hour. By the time Chuck left, his wages had risen to (an amazing) $8.00/hour. Chuck left the nursing job to work for his mother-in-law as a Prenney's security guard, earning $5.35/hour. I asked Chuck why he left the better-paying job at the nursing home and he shrugged, "Just got tired of it." After staying at Prenney's for a year, he left to take a job as a security guard at Eastside Mall, which paid $7.20/hour. Chuck was laid off after six months, but left at $7.50/hour. He was unemployed for four months, until he took a job selling vacuum cleaners that lasted a month—a job he recalls with lots of humor. He then began cooking burgers at the Red Coffee Pot, where he stayed for six months earning $4.35/hour. Chuck got his break when his uncle suggested he come work for Megamodal, where he was able to get a job as a warehouse man and janitor. He started at $5.50 and ended (several months later) at $6.75/hour when he was laid off. His father (a long-time Flacks employee) then helped him get a job at Flacks, a supplier of bar and restaurant supplies. He stayed for eleven months, starting at $5.50/hour and leaving at $5.75/hour. By the time of our interview, Chuck was working as a driver for Silters, which supplies and distributes cigarettes, candy, and fundraiser supplies. Chuck got this job indirectly through the Flacks job, where Silters often provided supplies. He was making $6.30/hour and driving his own car to work, about fifteen minutes away. He said he loved driving the large trucks, even on the crowded city route that he's been assigned, and hoped to stay much longer than he has at any other job. Chuck's experience suggests a haphazard pattern with lots of curves but considerable resilience. The final category is Low Success, perhaps better understood as an at-risk category—in which young men founder in minimum wage jobs, experience significant spells of unemployment, and at times fall into the discouraged worker category.

Low Success

A Low Success path includes some combination of the following characteristics: unemployment at the time of the interview and/or additional periods of significant unemployment (of at least three months' duration), underemployment (as indicated by a number of low-paying jobs in the formal or informal sectors, exclusively part-time work, or full-time work held only for short periods (usually less than three months), or consistent employment outside of the initial field of interest with few, if any, wage increases. These young men have not earned wages above $5.00/hour. Their postsecondary educational experiences are few, if any, and have not included two- or four-year colleges, significant on-the-job training, or any form of employer-sponsored coursework. Only a few black (7) and white (5) men fell into the low success category. Among the white men, Tim's experiences are typical.

Although Tim started out studying auto mechanics while in high school, he never held a job in that field. Tim's pattern exhibits a kind of frenetic activity that might be attributed to his musical aspirations, which seem to make other types of work boring for him. He left three jobs quickly as a teenager: at fourteen or fifteen he worked for the Red Coffee Pot ($3.35/hour) for three weeks; at sixteen his cousin's boyfriend hired him to work at Pizzaweel ($4.35/hour), where he stayed for two months; finally, during the summer after graduation, Tim worked at Stone's Supermarket ($5.65/hour) for four months and then took a month off. Tim then found a job at a Record House store through friends he knew who worked there. He stayed for almost three years, starting at $3.35/hour and ending at $6.50/hour. At that point, Tim quit the record store job and worked on the Harbor Shuttle Water Taxi for a summer at $5.00/hour. Just about one month before our interview, Tim had begun working at his friend's brother's restaurant, the Casual Cafe, where he earns $200/week waiting on people and assisting his friend, the manager. He drives his car five minutes to work. He mentioned that sometime after graduating, he went to community college for a semester to study criminal justice, but has not been able to work part-time and go to college as he had initially planned to do after graduating from Glendale. Tim's trajectory has been uncertain, and he expressed some concern about getting his music career off the ground. He expected to be working at the restaurant until he could figure out an entry point into the local musical scene, and hinted that some of his informal earning practices were just south of legal.

One black student, Jerome, shared Tim's inauspicious beginnings. Though by no means the only student with an incarceration record, Jerome, a talented mechanic, seemed headed nowhere fast when I interviewed him. Jerome studied accounting in high school and at the time of our interview was unemployed, having just gotten out of a one-year jail term for possession with intent to distribute cocaine. He admits to having been a bit of a troublemaker in high school, but, by his account and that of other students, he is a talented mechanic and only engaged in adolescent pranks in school. Jerome held a work-study job at Wald's department store during eleventh grade, then in twelfth grade he snagged a job as a mechanic's helper at Turner Station (he couldn't recall his wages at either of these jobs). After graduating, he worked full-time as a mechanic's helper at Davie's Auto Shop for $4.25/hour. A neighbor introduced Jerome to Davie and they got along fairly well, but Jerome says that he was fired from Davie's because of a discrepancy over missing parts. The last job Jerome held before going to prison was at Motors Unlimited, where he earned $420.00/week as a full-time mechanic's helper. At the time we spoke, Jerome hoped to find a job working as a mechanic soon but worried that his prison record could hurt him badly. I asked Jerome about his illegal earnings, but he had trouble estimating them, mainly because he said he had spent them nearly as quickly as he had earned them. He said that it was possible to earn up to $2,000/week selling cocaine in Baltimore if one could resist becoming a user in the process. While Jerome had not become a user, he had only engaged in casual dealing, which made getting caught all the more painful. Jerome's efforts to re-enter the auto mechanics field seem unpromising. Although his skills as a mechanic seem to have opened up opportunities in the past, Jerome has had no formal training and now has a criminal record that will have to be reported on job applications. As I left the interview, I kept my fingers crossed that Jerome — a quiet but candid young man — would be able to resist the lure of Baltimore's dangerous illegal economy.

One set of men in the study occupied an interesting position vis-à-vis their more work-bound peers — I labeled these men Miscellaneous because their main activities since graduating were in schools rather than jobs. None had worked full-time, and each seemed to be pursuing a career that would take him far away from the skilled trades arena. In some ways they became the extraneous category in this study — a category that would have been hard to analyze given the years of additional schooling each young man was determined to get.

Miscellaneous

Miscellaneous students generally were pursuing higher education in a way that indicated some level of career postponement, sometimes involuntary. A number of the men in this category attempted to get jobs right after graduating from high school but were unable to do so and decided to commit to further postsecondary training. In most cases, they were engaged simultaneously in schooling and part-time work that was not specifically related to their original training field. These students expected their schooling efforts to translate into better opportunities after graduation, usually in professional or managerial jobs. Most of the men in this category did not consider their current part-time jobs a part of their past or future career trajectories and hoped that I would not label them according to the temporary jobs that they held while pursuing higher degrees. For these reasons, I tend to think of these students as having delayed trajectories that are perhaps best not examined alongside the other men's patterns.

Who Landed Where?

Having determined a set of success categories, the question that remains is who — in terms of race — landed where? Table 2 shows black and white men's success categories by field status (within or outside). This table summarizes some of the patterns we will be unraveling in future chapters.

Table 2. *Black and White Men's Success Categories by Field Status*

Success Category	Within Field	Outside Field
High		
Black men	1	3
White men	6	10
Moderate		
Black men	1	9
White men	2	1
Low		
Black men	0	4
White men	0	1

Miscellaneous category is excluded from table. Chi-square test for significance for this distribution (of a nonrandom sample of this size) exceeded .05 significance level.

Table 2 highlights a number of racially divergent patterns that are alarming and demand analysis. First, the table demonstrates that whites in this study are about three times more likely than blacks to experience highly successful school-to-work transitions. Second, the table shows that white men's chances of creating stable trajectories within their vocational fields or of successfully switching fields after graduating are vastly better than black males' chances. Third, while black men were slightly more likely to have achieved moderate rather than low success, moderate success trajectories most often involved abandoning original trade fields for less remunerative service sector opportunities; only white males seemed consistently able to switch from one blue-collar field to another. Only one white graduate fit the Low Success criteria, as opposed to five black graduates. These patterns might be surprising if large-scale representative samples didn't point to identical types of outcomes at the national level.[13] How can we explain these divergent trajectories among men who had nearly identical beginnings and who demonstrated academic persistence and trade competencies that should have made them equally employable? In the next chapter, we'll evaluate how additional data on these young men compare to the reigning Market explanations — explanations that are thought to capture common sense on one hand and uncommon insight on the other.

FIVE

Evaluating Market Explanations

*The Declining Significance of Race
and Racial Deficits Approaches*

The data in Chapter 4 indicate major racial differences in early employment outcomes, but either of two factors could mitigate our concerns about the discriminatory implications of those differences: (1) things are bad, but getting better — these findings indicate progress or (2) these unequal outcomes among Glendale graduates are justified because of *hidden* differences in school performance, motivation, and character — characteristics on the basis of which employers have the right to make decisions — so unequal outcomes do not indicate unfair discrimination. These positions hearken back to the two types of market explanations that I discussed in Chapter 2; one is William Julius Wilson's Declining Significance of Race, the other is the Racial Deficits approach that is thought to reflect common sense. Though not often seen this way, Wilson's claims in the *Declining Significance of Race* identify his position within the Market approach, which sees human capital (skills and experiences) as far more significant than race in predicting the life chances of young blacks. Because Wilson argues that race has declined in significance *only since the Civil Rights era*, to examine his thesis appropriately, it is necessary to locate data from two specific time periods, prior to and after the Civil Rights movement. In the first section of this chapter, I compare data from a study conducted in Baltimore in the early 1960s with my 1990s data, to determine whether differentials in earnings and employment rates remained the same, increased, or decreased for black and white men with the same educational credentials. If the differentials decreased over time for these men with equivalent human capital, then Wilson's Declining Significance of Race thesis is supported for the black working-class men I studied. If, as I will demonstrate, the differentials remained roughly equivalent or increased, then Wilson's thesis would not be supported and — at least based on these data — race cannot be said to have declined in significance as a factor affecting the life chances of the black working class. Because the differences observed between white and black working-class men resemble differences found between poor blacks and whites, labor market disadvantages that Wilson associates solely with ghetto residence appear to be more applicable than expected to working-class blacks who are not ghetto residents. I save this interpretation for the last section of the chapter. In the second section, I compare the black and white men of my study with respect to an additional set of variables — character, motivation, and school-related characteristics — that are sometimes thought to be important for explaining differential employment outcomes among similarly educated black and white men. If the white men have better grades and attendance or are more committed to hard work, then the Racial Deficits perspective might provide a credible explanation for differential employment success, even among workers who appear educationally equivalent.

THE SIGNIFICANCE OF RACE

In an earlier chapter, I briefly mentioned a study of school-work transition that was conducted in Baltimore in the early 1960s by Johns Hopkins University researchers Edmund D. Meyers, Jr. and Yvonne Hajda, under the direction of Bernard Levenson and James Coleman. Their report began:

Since its inception the Equal Opportunity Commission has been interested in assembling facts bearing on the relative employment and earnings of Negroes and whites in the Baltimore community. That Negroes in the United States have considerably lower earnings than whites and considerably higher rates of unemployment is, of course, well-documented. But the question that is not satisfactorily answered — and one on which the direction of social and legal efforts depends — is how much of the inequality results from patent discrimination by employers (and unions and employment agencies) and how much from discrimination in the quantity and quality of education that Negroes receive vis a vis whites? For it is also well-documented that, on the average, Negro students receive fewer years of formal education in schools that are characteristically inferior in staff and facilities to those available for whites.[1]

Meyers and Hajda then went on to describe how the Equal Opportunity Commission asked a group of sociologists to conduct a systematic study of the employment opportunities of Negroes and whites in Baltimore. Using earnings and employment data from the Social Security Administration, Meyers and Hajda obtained information for nine graduating classes of Glendale and Wakefield Vocational-Technical High Schools in Baltimore. At the time, 98 percent of the students at Glendale were white, while Wakefield was an all-black school. The high schools had comparable facilities and were staffed by teachers who conformed to the same training standards. Consequently, Meyer and Hajda argued that "extreme differences in the employment and earnings of the students of the two schools would suggest differential treatment by employment agencies, unions or employers, or that the vocational guidance and placement programs warrant re-appraisal."[2]

Meyer and Hajda also outlined parameters of their study that mirror my own: (1) they included only high school graduates; (2) they included both students who no longer lived in the city and those who had joined the armed services; and (3) they looked at only the first few years after the students graduated. In addition, Meyer and Hajda purposely omitted students who did not have social security numbers and those who had no earnings; I found myself forced to do so as well.

Unlike my study, Meyer and Hajda's study examined the employment trajectories of the young men at three-month intervals; my data did not allow for quarterly comparisons. Another difference involved Meyer and Hajda's choice to exclude students who had pursued trades that were unavailable to one or the other set of students. The twelve trades that were common to both schools included auto mechanics, carpentry, commercial art, electrical construction and maintenance, food preparation and service, machine shop, tool and die making, radio, television, and electronics, trowel trades, welding, business education, cosmetology, and dressmaking. (The last three categories were thought of as "female trades.") Among male-dominated trades, only Wakefield, the black school, taught dry cleaning and pressing, painting and paperhanging, shoe repair, and tailoring and design, while only Glendale, the white school, offered aircraft and general sheet metal, airplane mechanics, commercial baking, industrial electronics, mechanical drafting and design, metal casting, oil burner installation, plumbing and heating, printing, and a technicians program.

Meyer and Hajda randomly selected 493 male students — 283 from Glendale and 210 from Wakefield — out of a total population of 1,044 students from the 1957–60 graduating classes. Four of the nine cohorts they examined graduated in January (1957–60) and five cohorts graduated in June (1956–60). Meyer and Hajda compared the median earnings and the overall employment rates for each of the nine cohorts over a set number of months. For the January graduates, they compared the men from one to twelve months after graduation and then again from thirteen to twenty-four months. For the June graduates, comparisons were made from seven to eighteen months after graduation. The guiding questions of the research concerned the ratio of black to white earnings over time.

In Meyer and Hajda's original 1969 report, black males were least likely to approach white males' earnings in their first twelve months in the labor force, when the first cohort of black students (January graduates [n = 57]) managed to earn only 54 percent of the median earnings of their white counterparts (n = 69). Among the June graduates, who make up a substantially larger group (n = 367) and who were examined seven to eighteen months after graduation, black men earned 68 percent of their white counterparts' median income. In their final comparison of the January graduates (from thirteen to twenty-four months after graduation), Meyer and Hajda found that the black/white median ratio had improved from the one-to-twelve-month 54 percent ratio to 67 percent. This finding indicates that black males appeared to get a slower start than white males, but over time they had the potential to catch up. At the same time, though, Meyer and Hajda pointed out that in no case were black workers of the same cohort on a par with their white counterparts, and even more disturbingly, even the earnings of white males who had been in the labor market for the shortest time (one to twelve months) generally exceeded the earnings of black males who had been in the labor market for the longest time (twenty-four months).

Meyer and Hajda also examined employment rates among the nine cohorts. Access to detailed social security records enabled them to look at employment rates during each of the first four quarters following graduation. The researchers felt confident that their reliance on social security records was far superior to the self-reports of graduates, whom they suggested would be "subject to all of the hazards of memory, fantasy, falsification, or bias."[3]

Even though Meyer and Hajda were correct to point out that self-reported data on earnings and employment may have been suspect, they did not consider the possibility that official reports leave out income that is earned "off-the-books" — thus social security figures probably underestimated the men's true earnings. These sorts of unreported wage supplements can be quite significant for working-class men who pursue side jobs, as many of my respondents did. If I had relied solely on social security records, a substantial amount of cash and in-kind transfers would have remained hidden. In my interviews, I learned that some of the most successful men relied almost completely on unreported earnings and informal bartering arrangements. Nevertheless, a combination of self-reported and official records would have been better than either measure alone for both studies.

Meyer and Hajda noted two patterns in their examination of black and white males' employment patterns: first, in both cases the men generally increased their rate of employment over time; second, the employment rates of the young men show greater parity than their median earnings ratios. By the fourth quarter, the weighted average employment rate for the nine cohorts was 93.3 percent. This means that, between 1957 and 1960, for every one hundred employed white males, there were at least ninety-three employed black males in this sample population — a very close rate, indeed. The earnings picture was not so rosy, however, since for every dollar earned by white males, black males earned only sixty-seven cents. Juxtaposing Meyer and Hajda's data and my own, it is possible to approximate how much has changed for vocationally trained black and white men in Baltimore over the last thirty-three to thirty-five years.

Data comparing median income and employment rate ratios for blacks and whites from Meyer and Hajda's 1957–60 study and my 1994 study, indicate a gain on one side and a loss on the other. Employed black men have increased their median earnings ratio from 67 percent in 1957–60 to 73 percent in 1994, a very modest 6 percent improvement in the black-white ratio. However, the black graduates in the early 1960s were employed at rates only 7 percent lower than their white counterparts, while the same black graduates, thirty-three to thirty-five years later, were employed 17 percent less often than their white counterparts, reflecting a 10 percent worsening in the black/white ratio over the same time period.

The gain (in wages) reflects an averaged increase of one-fifth of one percent (0.2 percent) per year. But the apparent increase should be interpreted cautiously for several reasons. The 1957–60 income ratios that

Meyer and Hajda observed in the first two years of the school-work transition might have reached or exceeded the 73 percent mark that I observed, had they continued collecting data three years into the transition process, as I did. In addition, when I compared the mean rather than median incomes, the black/white income ratio declined to 63 percent. Relying on median income for comparisons reduces the significance of the cases at either extreme and may in some ways be misleading, in this case minimizing the influence of five black respondents who had no earnings at the time of my interviews. Finally, the apparent increase in wage ratios can be better understood if we examine it in the context of increases from other time periods. According to Meyer and Hajda,

> the gap between Negro and white males started to narrow during World War II as a result for *[sic]* the demand for skilled and semi-skilled labor in the defense plants and as a result of federal influence on policies of employment. And for the first time, Negro males secured skilled jobs from which they had generally been excluded, such as welders, machinists, electricians, etc. During the last two decades [1940–1960] the narrowing has amounted to slightly less than 20%: from 1939 to 1947 it narrowed by about 1.5% per year; from 1947 to 1960, by almost .5 % per year.[4]

Meyer and Hajda's figures indicate that earnings converged at a faster rate prior to the Civil Rights movement than they did after the movement. Sadly, this finding, and the finding that employment rates were more similar in the pre– rather than post–Civil Rights era, provide only minimal support for Wilson's Declining Significance of Race thesis for the black working class.[5] The pace of black gains is so slow as to suggest that working-class black men cannot now expect to achieve the same earnings or employment rate as their comparably educated white peers any more than they could thirty years ago.

Meyer and Hajda, who, incidentally, found even greater disparity among the female cohorts than the male cohorts in their 1957–60 study, expressed concern that whites' greater success in the labor market might be interpreted as evidence of blacks' inferiority. They concluded:

Undoubtedly, some will attribute these differences to "cultural deprivation." This is another way of saying that Negroes come from
unwholesome environments, that their parents have little formal
schooling, that they lack initiative and ambition, that they are not
reliable or punctual, etc. More candid discussions may produce
items such as neglected teeth, matters of personal hygiene, stealing,
etc. Undoubtedly, some of these factors play a role in getting a job
and holding a job: they need to be investigated."[6]

My intention, in the next section, is to take up their challenge.

DIFFERENTIAL ABILITIES AND RACIAL DEFICITS: TAKING CONSERVATIVE CONCERNS SERIOUSLY

> Most employers now pay blacks who can talk, think, and act like
> whites almost as much as they pay "real whites."
>
> — Christopher Jencks

According to market perspectives, differential employment outcomes
are generally a function of the differential educational, skill, and experience backgrounds — human capital — and work orientations (willingness
to work hard, for example) of workers. When women and minority men
earn less money and hold less power as workers than white men, the
market perspective answers that such differences are probably justified
by virtue of white men's superior education, training, relevant work
skills, and/or pro-work values. A number of large-scale studies that use
nationally representative samples consistently find that white male high
school graduates earn more than black male high school graduates, even
when the influence of relevant factors, such as work-orientation, is held
constant.[7] Since internal factors do not explain differences in work outcomes, factors external to black workers themselves, such as racial discrimination, are thought to account for the differences.[8]

But the Market approach suggests alternative explanations here: instead of racism, significant differences in the *quality* of education acquired

by white and black high school graduates could account for unequal out-comes, or other differences connected to character and motivation, or inadequately measured dimensions of work orientation, might explain them.

The argument that a high school degree earned by a black male may not be the real equivalent of the same degree earned by a white male takes at least two forms. Proponents of this position do not necessarily imply that blacks are intellectually inferior to whites, nor do they neces-sarily suggest that black and white diploma holders are not functionally equivalent. It could be that the schools attended by most whites are superior to the schools attended by most blacks; therefore, on average, white male high school graduates have a qualitatively superior educa-tion — a more valuable diploma, if you will, than blacks.[9] In my study, this issue is rendered irrelevant by the fact that all the men attended the same school. A second argument suggests that having an equivalent number of years of education and even graduating from the same insti-tution are crude measures of equivalence that could hide equally, if not more important, traits, such as grades, difficulty of courses taken, and standardized test scores.[10] This argument is worth exploring further.

For younger workers, human capital is usually operationalized using measures of students' academic achievements, such as achievement test scores and grades. Vocational students, unlike those in college prepara-tory tracks, are unlikely to take a battery of tests, like SATs and ACTs, since they do not usually plan to attend competitive colleges after grad-uating. Although some of the young men in the study did take the SATs, the measures most consistently available for the vast majority of the young men were scores from reading and math proficiency tests taken prior to the twelfth grade, along with their cumulative grade point aver-ages. Comparing these measures could shed some light on why employ-ment outcomes diverged. If, for example, the blacks in the study were, on average, D students and the whites were, on average, A students, or if the blacks' reading or math proficiency levels were well below those of the whites, then it would make sense to argue that the whites' superior mastery of subject matter explains at least part — and possibly all — of the difference in employment experience. Such findings would lend empirical support to the notion that diplomas earned by blacks do not represent the same accomplishments as diplomas earned by whites.

Other types of arguments hearken back to the Cultural Deprivation explanation mentioned by Meyer and Hajda and the Racial Deficits approaches of conservative scholars such as Dinesh D'Souza, Lawrence Mead, and Charles Murray. These sorts of arguments are founded on the notion that blacks do indeed "come from unwholesome environments, that their parents have little formal schooling, that they lack initiative and ambition, that they are not reliable or punctual, etc." — concerns Meyer and Hajda were worried, in the 1960s, would distract from efforts to dismantle the influence of racial barriers. Such characteristics, though not strictly measures of educational qualifications, nonetheless remain troubling concerns for urban employers and others.[11] As such, I consider their influence, as well as the influence of more traditional educational achievement variables, in the section that follows.

In the structured portion of my interviews, I asked a number of questions that tapped into issues relevant to the different types of market arguments. Specifically, I examined a set of twenty variables under three categories: academic, character, and motivation/preparedness. The academic category includes more traditional educational measures, while the character and motivation/preparedness categories include behaviors and attitudes that address the validity of commonly held negative stereotypes about young working-class black men — their alleged racial deficits. Given the earnings and employment rate advantage, as well as the higher overall levels of success, of the whites in the study, it seems reasonable to ask whether the whites shared certain characteristics that might explain their relative advantage. For example, maybe those who succeeded worked harder or were more diligent or responsible — some will undoubtedly wonder if they were just smarter. Using information from their school records and from the interviews, it is possible to examine these sorts of questions.

Academic

I sought variables that could serve as indicators of students' academic achievements, ultimately choosing to include the students' grade point averages (available for all fifty students) over their four-year high school career (scale 0–100); math and reading scores from standardized achievement tests (for math, n = 34; for reading, n = 42) taken prior to the twelfth grade; the combined number of years of schooling for the mother and father (range 1–18 for each parent); whether (according to the young men's self-reports) school personnel offered to write recommendation letters for the students, make phone calls to employers, or serve as a reference if necessary; whether school personnel ever suggested that students continue their education beyond high school (such as community college, university, apprenticeship or internship, or a specialized trade or technical school); and finally their vocational fields. While grades and test results certainly provide one measure of competence, school staff willingness to recommend students and confidence that students should pursue additional education at the postsecondary level are also indicators of student competence, and perhaps maturity.

Early studies of male mobility usually included at least one measure of parental educational level, usually relying solely on the father's educational level. The rationale for including parents' educational level (and sometimes linking it to a child's potential ability) was probably based on at least two assumptions: (1) that parents' educational achievements — even crudely measured by years of education — somehow convey advantages to children, and (2) that the educational levels reached by parents are an indicator of children's educational potential. Although I am more inclined toward the former assumption, I include the parental education measure, combining mother's and father's total years of schooling (including postsecondary technical school years, as well as years in junior and four-year colleges) at least in part because the argument has been made, as Meyer and Hajda pointed out, that black parents may have little formal schooling and thus have little to pass on to their chil-

Table 3. *Academic Characteristics*

Academic Measures	Black Students	White Students
Grades (GPA out of 100)	77.74	78.68
Math tests (% score)	83.88 (n = 16)	82.61 (n = 18)
Reading tests (% score)	77.00 (n = 20)	79.90 (n = 22)
Parents' education (years)	24.46	21.56
Offered recommendation	76%	72%
Suggested for college	44%	48%
Fields:		
Auto mechanics/body	8	5
Electrical construction	4	5
Business/related	4	3
Electronics (incl. industrial)	3	3
Printing	1	2
Trowel trades	1	2
Drafting	0	3
Machine shop	0	2
Carpentry	2	0
Food services	2	0

dren in terms of academic skills or assistance. I also include the fields the young men studied in the achievement category because significant differences in the courses of study chosen by black and white males could be a reason for employment differentials.

From Table 3, we see that neither the grades nor the math and reading competencies of the black and white students is very different. The blacks' grade point average is 77.74 and the whites' is 78.68, or a high C average; the blacks' math competency average was 83.88, while the whites' was 82.61; and the reading score average for the blacks was 77.00, while the whites averaged 79.9. On all three measures, the young men's scores were quite close. Similarly, virtually identical percentages of the young men said that school personnel offered to write them letters of recommendation or suggested that they attend college — 76 percent of the black males and 72 percent of the white males were offered recommendations and 44 percent of the black males and 48 percent of the white males were told to continue their education. Perhaps surprisingly, the black men's parents had, on average, almost three more years of formal schooling than the white men's parents. This suggests that it is unlikely that black parents' education levels in any way worsened their son's employment prospects.

Although my sampling technique was not designed to match the young men by vocational fields, most of the young men were concentrated in the same fields: 32 percent of black males and 20 percent of white males chose auto mechanics or auto body shop; 16 percent of black males and 20 percent of white males chose electrical construction; 16 percent of black males and 12 percent of white males chose business related fields; and 12 percent of black and white males chose electronics. Only two black men (8 percent) chose food services, a field that is not usually considered a traditional male or male-dominated field. Over 90 percent of the black and white men chose vocational concentrations that were in traditional, male-dominated fields where wages usually exceed those in the minimum wage secondary service sector. This indicates that the vocational fields chosen by black men did not worsen their employment prospects. In short, none of the traditional academic measures associated with the human-capital perspective can explain the earnings and employment rate differentials found among these young men.

Character

For a number of years, perhaps since the public became concerned with social scientific evidence regarding the urban underclass in the latter part of the 1980s, urban employers, conservative social scholars, and ordinary people have exhibited concern that black men, particularly those who live in cities, may not have developed the sort of character traits that make them good employees.[12] It seems plausible to ask whether the young black and white men in this study have markedly different character traits. I identified five variables that could be used as indicators of behavioral proclivities and work orientations that might differentiate blacks and whites: the percentage of students who reported significant trouble with teachers, the percentage of students who admitted to having been arrested or incarcerated, the lowest wage the men said they would accept if they were unemployed (reservation wage), the number who had held jobs in low-status, service sector jobs, and the percentage who would refuse to take jobs in low-prestige fields. Specifically, trouble with instructors was a self-report item worded, "Did you ever encounter trouble with your main instructors that might have made them unlikely to suggest you for specific jobs or as a work-study candidate?"; trouble with police was measured by an affirmative answer to the question, "Have you been arrested or incarcerated for illegal activities?"; lowest acceptable wage was measured by the question, "How much money would a job have to offer before you would take it?"; whether students had held low-prestige jobs was answered affirmatively if the student had ever held a low-status, minimum- or subminimum-wage job in the low-level service sector — busboys, dishwashers, fast-food jobs, etc.; and percentages who would refuse jobs in certain fields was created by listing all of the jobs the men mentioned when asked, "What kinds of jobs would you refuse to take?" and then tabulating the answers for the most common responses, namely, fast-food, janitorial, sales, cleaning, food-oriented, and heavy lifting. The results are found in Table 4.

With regard to behavioral proclivities, in neither case could the majority of young men be seen as troublemakers. There was only one measure that was significantly worse for blacks than whites — 16 percent of black men reported having had difficult interactions with teachers that might have affected teachers' willingness to help them with employment, while only 4 percent of white males had. Conversely, 20 percent of the white males in the study said they'd been arrested, while only 12 percent of the black men had. This statistic is perhaps surprising because it goes against national statistics, but it must be kept in mind that the

Table 4. *Character-Oriented Characteristics*

Character measures	Black Students	White Students
Trouble with instructors	16%	4%
Trouble with police	12%	20%
Reservation wage	$6.28	$7.86
Had held low-prestige job*	76%	44%
Jobs would refuse:		
Fast-food*	32%	60%
Janitorial	12%	12%
Sales*	12%	40%
Cleaning	20%	28%
Food-oriented	8%	24%
Heavy lifting	8%	4%

Significance levels *<.05 based on two-sample tests of proportions.

black respondents in this study are not (yet) members of any type of urban underclass—most, like their white peers, live with their stably employed parents, in modest but comfortable homes. The black men's behavioral measures indicate that only a small percentage ever encountered serious trouble with either their teachers or the police. Because the white men's percentages are similar, again it would seem that behavioral differences do not account for the differentials in earnings and employment rate.

Work orientation seems especially important. All too familiar are the media's pronouncements that young American workers are unwilling to work at "honest" jobs just because the wages that are offered to them in such jobs are low and their trajectories are not promising. Supposedly, they are unwilling to work their way up and would rather have no job than a poorly paid job in a low-prestige field. Young minority workers are particularly vulnerable to this stereotype. Yet the black males in the study were willing to accept wages (mean = $6.28) more than $1.50

lower than the white males (mean = $7.86) in this study. It may be that white males — who had higher employment rates as well as earnings — had come to expect higher wages, but clearly this pattern does not support the general stereotype that is applied to black male workers who live in the inner city.

In addition, black men were more, rather than less, likely to have taken or be willing to take the sorts of jobs that are routinely considered "too dirty" or "dead-end" for most American workers. Thus 76 percent of the black males in the study had (past age 16) held a job in the least desirable portions of the service sector, while only 44 percent of white males had done so. Perhaps most telling of all are the types of jobs that the men would refuse: at the time of the interviews, 60 percent of the white males would refuse fast food employment, while only 32 percent of black males would; 12 percent of white and black males would refuse janitorial work; 40 percent of white males would refuse any sort of sales work, as compared to only 12 percent of black men; 20 percent of black men would refuse work that required cleaning, while 28 percent of white males would refuse such jobs; three times as many white males (24 percent) as black males (8 percent) would refuse any food-oriented job; finally, only jobs involving heavy lifting were less desirable to black men (8 percent) than to white men (4 percent). None of these findings suggests that black men have a poor work orientation in comparison to white men, nor are the differences found here in work orientation directionally consistent with the earnings and employment rate differentials.

Motivation/Preparedness

Another set of characteristics that is rarely included in large-scale studies, motivation/preparedness factors, allowed me to look into some of the issues that concern those who argue the potentially negative influence of black cultural practices. I see these variables as indicative of motivation and preparedness because each provides a glimpse of the young men's sense of responsibility and initiative and their level of commitment to becoming successfully employed. For example, employers expect employees to be dependable, and high attendance (measured by thirty or fewer absences in the four-year high school career) seems a logical predictor for reliably showing up for work. If black males have attendance problems that white males don't exhibit, then this factor could surely explain part of the difference in early work experiences. I also asked as a measure of preparedness whether the men had resumes at the time of the interview. Another question — "Have you had any formal training since leaving Glendale (college, technical school, army, special training, etc.)?" — was designed to examine whether young men demonstrated motivation and commitment to acquiring new work skills. Clearly, if white males are more committed than black males to skill enhancement, this could account for employment differences. Other questions tapped into how willing young men were to persist through transportation obstacles to find work. I asked, "How far would you be willing to travel to work for the right job?" and whether the young men had ever walked or taken the bus to work.

Another measure that labor market researchers frequently use asks subjects to evaluate a list of reasons for quitting a job. From subjects' choices, we get a very good idea of what is considered tolerable and intolerable in the work setting. Certainly it could be the case that black workers don't do as well because their expectations in the work setting are unrealistically high vis-à-vis the expectations of their white peers. I tabulated the reasons to quit that each man selected, and then averaged the choices by group. They included:

> 1. wages were too low; 2. you didn't like the people you worked
> with; 3. you didn't like the customers or clients; 4. you had an illness;
> 5. a family member had an illness; 6. you wanted to return to school;
> 7. your friends didn't respect you for working there; 8. you didn't
> like the kind of work; 9. you needed to take a break; 10. you found
> another job; 11. you wanted to look for another job; 12. child care
> was a problem; 13. you had to travel too much or too far to work;
> 14. you felt uncomfortable or out of place there; 15. the hours were
> bad; 16. the work was dangerous; 17. the work was beneath the posi-

Table 5. *Motivation and Preparedness Characteristics*

Motivation/Preparedness Measures	Black Students	White Students
Had resume	32%	32%
High attendance	68%	48%
Attempted work-study	72%	76%
Attempted post-high school training	68%	60%
Willing to travel to work (minutes)	78.64	55.20
Took bus or walked to work*	44%	12%
Reasons to quit (out of 20)	8.32	7.28
Nuclear family	60%	84%

Significance levels *<.05 based on two-sample tests of proportions.

tion you deserved; 18. the job had no future; 19. you experienced harassment from your boss; 20. you experienced harassment from other workers.

I included one other variable in the motivation/preparedness category: family configuration. While conservatives would tend to argue that being raised in a single-parent household (the assumption of illegitimate birth nearly automatic) is inherently less desirable from a moral standpoint, I think a more plausible concern is whether having two parents around to support and/or pressure youth in the job search may be more helpful than just one. On the other hand, an equally plausible argument can be made that young men who have single parents, particularly single mothers, feel an even stronger motivation or pressure than men from two-parent families to become employed as soon as possible in order to assist with the family's overall bread-winning scheme. For these reasons, I hesitate to interpret the importance of family configuration as an explanatory variable. The results of the comparison of motivation and preparedness measures are included in Table 5.

In the case of some of the less ambiguous measures, patterns in this category mirror those found in the academic and character categories.

That is, in no cases are black men lagging substantially behind their white peers and in some cases they appear to be more impressive from a prospective employer's likely standpoint, stereotypes notwithstanding. A mere 32 percent of the black and white males had resumes at the time of the interview, but the black men (68 percent) were much more likely than the white males (48 percent) to have high attendance rates. A similar percentage of black men (72 percent) and white men (76 percent) attempted to get into work-study programs while they were in high school, and a similar number attempted to attain some type of post–high school training. A comparable 68 percent of black males and 60 percent of white males had attempted to further their education since leaving high school. The percentage for the black men is especially significant because black men were more likely to pay for their post–secondary training, while the white men in this study frequently received training subsidized by their employers. In a similar vein, black men were willing to travel over twenty minutes longer to work (mean = 78.64 minutes) than their white peers (mean = 55.20 minutes). But this comparison may not be completely fair to white men, who might be willing to travel an equal distance to work but be able to get there faster because they have their own means of transportation. In other words, because black men in this study are less likely to have access to private transportation, they may expect to take more time to get to work as a result of relying on public transport. A related measure, which is less relevant for the white males in this study, is whether the men have ever taken the bus or walked to work. A much higher percentage of black men (44 percent) had walked or taken the bus to work compared to white males (12 percent), who were more likely to have gotten first vehicles while still in their teens. This measure shows that, despite transportation difficulties, a significant number of young black men demonstrated a willingness to use public transportation or to walk to jobs. Finally, black men selected a slightly higher number of reasons to quit a job (mean = 8.32) than white males (mean = 7.28) out of the twenty offered in the interview schedule. Interestingly, this difference could have resulted from one reason that nearly every white male ruled out, namely child care. It seems that the white males in the study could not conceive of child care concerns as a reason for quitting a job. This is perhaps not surprising, since the overwhelming majority of white males in the study had mothers who were housewives, and several expressed the hope that their own wives would not have to work outside of the home. Incidentally, none of the men had any child care concerns yet, though a few had children (the same number of black and white men were fathers). With regard to the nuclear family measures, not surprisingly, given recent studies of race and marital patterns, fewer of the black men's families (60 percent) fell into the nuclear configuration compared to the white men (84 percent). Is this a source of white men's labor market advantages? Perhaps. Although parental configuration seems to me to be more directly related to the immediately available resources of a student or the potential life stressors (parents separating or divorcing) faced by students, market-oriented arguments continue to suggest that nuclear families are more able to instill values and behaviors that stress responsibility and initiative and that even those who do not instill such values by example do so by providing effective sanctions against irresponsible behavior or low initiative. The results seem unclear on this point, but overall, there seems little reason to draw the conclusion that differences in the motivation or preparedness of the black and white men in this study accounted for their differential employment success. It seems, judging from the full set of measures, that the young black men have similar academic achievements, character traits, and motivation/preparedness characteristics as their white counterparts while more often living in single-parent families. Further, I am aware of no studies that compare the employment motivation of young men living in nuclear versus single-parent households, and without such data, there is no compelling reason to follow one line of logic rather than another.

To summarize, on most of the measures, the black and white men in this study demonstrated similar academic, character, and motivation/preparedness levels. In only two cases were the black men seriously lagging behind the white men, namely in the percentage having had trouble with instructors and in family configuration. In several cases, the black men's qualities should have put them at an advantage when compared to their white peers. Taken as a whole, in eighteen of twenty market-oriented variables, the black and white men in this study were virtually indistinguishable, or the black men showed a slight advantage. Yet, despite these important similarities, neither the earnings nor the employment rate of the black men is comparable to that of the white men. Instead, black men have lost ground since the 1960s in terms of overall employment rate, and their earnings have risen at a rate lower than in the pre–Civil Rights period. These findings are even more troubling when we recall that these are the young people who have done what society suggests they should: they have stayed in school, taken the "dirty" jobs, gone to school regularly, performed at a satisfactory level, stayed out of police trouble, and impressed school personnel. They have followed the rules, and yet they have been unable to get returns on their educational and behavioral investments comparable to those of their white peers. These findings suggest that market variables — human capital and character/motivation factors — cannot explain differences in the early employment trajectories of the white and black men in this study.

Ghetto Results Without Ghetto Residence

In terms of the experiences of the working class black men in this study, William Julius Wilson's arguments concerning the employment difficulties of male ghetto residents seem more relevant and applicable than his arguments concerning well-educated blacks. According to Wilson, black ghetto residents, especially males, face considerable disadvantages in the labor market, which are the result of the tremendous loss of manufacturing jobs within central cities and social and geographic isolation in the poorest, most underserved, and under-resourced neighborhoods. These factors, Wilson argues, exacerbate insufficient job networks, a lack of transportation, and a set of negative stereotypes held by urban employers. Presumably because white males — even poor ones — do not live in comparably isolated ghettos within central cities, they suffer fewer of the problems (poor contacts, insufficient transportation, and negative stereotypes) that plague poor black men and contribute to severe employment problems. Yet, without living in ghetto neighborhoods or being at any distinct disadvantage in schooling or character vis-à-vis their white peers, the working-class black men I studied demonstrated employment problems more similar to their poorer and more socially and geographically isolated black peers than to their same-class white peers. The relative affluence of black working-class parents (vis-à-vis poor blacks) does not seem to increase the employment possibilities of their sons — even those who play by the rules. This suggests that ghetto residence — social and geographic isolation — may be sufficient to insure severe employment difficulties among black men, but it is, disturbingly, not necessary. As I have shown in this chapter, black working class men suffer employment difficulties unrelated to ability or character even if they do not live in the ghetto. The three black disadvantages — lack of networks, lack of transportation, and the presence of discrimination — operate irrespective of class and residential advantages associated with being a member of the stable working or lower-middle class.

SIX

Embedded Transitions

School Ties
and the Unanticipated Significance of Race

In the post–Civil Rights era, schools have come to be seen as institutions that are capable of and committed to endowing dedicated students, irrespective of race, with skills and experiences that enable all to compete fairly for the rewards of the greater society. In addition to their preparatory role, schools are also expected to contribute to allocation — specifically, selecting and sorting young people towards appropriate post-schooling opportunities, again irrespective of race. If either the preparatory or the allocational functions are subverted in the interests of a dominant racial group, then the schools' function as an equalizing institution is undermined from within, and schools reinforce the infrastructure of unearned racial privilege that they could instead be disassembling.

In Chapter 5, similar patterns of academic accomplishment among the men I studied indicate that the schools my subjects attended, including Glendale, provided similar subject mastery. This is a laudable preparatory accomplishment, but the question that still must be addressed is whether unequal employment outcomes resulted (at least in part) from failures in the school's function of allocation — which is less directly under the control of the school than the preparatory function, and more influenced by the social customs of city residents, historical ties with employers, and the informal placement practices of school personnel. In this chapter, I examine the racial embeddedness of Glendale and how that embeddedness has affected its allocation function, specifically its status or reputation among white city residents, its ability to maintain contacts with local employers, and its internal job placement mechanisms.

THROUGH THE LENS OF RACE: GLENDALE'S CHANGING INSTITUTIONAL STATUS

Students often attempt to affiliate themselves with prestigious educational institutions (as well as individuals) to better their chances of gaining entry into desirable occupations within desirable organizations. Frequently students compete against one another for high-status internships, scholarships, and extracurricular experiences that convey ambition and intellectual promise. Students who have a good understanding of the process presumably have an advantage over those whose choices are more random. These sorts of institution selection and portfolio building activities are most often associated with college-bound students, who spend considerable time attempting to choose the most useful courses of study within the best available high schools in order to be able to enter the most prestigious colleges and universities. Students, both consciously and unconsciously, strategize to be accepted to the better colleges because they believe that such colleges provide superior training (human capital), superior faculty, administrative, and peer networks (social capital), and superior exposure to elite liberal arts subject matter (cultural capital). For such students, establishing institutional affiliations is an important part of building human, social, and cultural capital to be exchanged later in the professional labor market.

Though the process of strategic institutional affiliation is somewhat different and usually truncated for work-bound students and working-class families, it is possible to identify similar selection criteria. For example, vocational students choose schools that are known to have good equipment and training, strong placement programs, and solid reputations among local employers. Because they are financially constrained, the families of work-bound students usually cannot afford to go very far beyond local areas to find more suitable educational facilities for their children. Despite this constraint, students often have some choice in terms of the institutions they attend, and many attempt to choose rationally, like their college-bound counterparts.

In my study, the choice to attend Glendale was made when the students were in the eighth grade. For some, the choice was complicated and difficult; for others it was as simple as attending the nearest neighborhood school. Almost uniformly, both black and white males and their families would have preferred suburban vocational schools, but only some white males insisted that they'd make sure their own children would never attend city schools like Glendale if they could avoid it. In the interviews, a pattern emerged in which white graduates and their families provided detailed and highly critical observations about Glendale, while black graduates and their families mainly offered neutral observations or mild praise. It became apparent that perceptions of Glendale were refracted through the lens of race. For some of the white students, attending Glendale was a family tradition, while for others it was a race-delineated compromise linked to their family's inability to leave Baltimore. For black students — only the second generation of nonwhite graduates — attending Glendale seemed a decidedly more positive option, not linked to financial hardship and based to some extent on Glendale's positive reputation.

The meaning of the Glendale choice for the white males and their families was also structured by race-based exclusionary patterns prevalent in Baltimore until the 1970s and more recent demographic changes that reversed the earlier patterns. In their critiques, white graduates and their families stressed the deterioration of Glendale in a number of areas. They mentioned reductions in the number of available trades, faulty and outdated equipment, missing and damaged equipment, reductions in teaching staff, and retirements among the best qualified teachers. They were also concerned about the increasing numbers of black students and staff. One student, Justin Guess, explained his reluctance to attend Glendale as a response to earlier negative experiences in a school with a high proportion of black students.

> I had some problems with racial things there because it [middle school] was all black. That's been a problem ever since I've been going to school except for when I went to Catonsville. Elementary school wasn't too bad, then middle school was real bad and I think that might be one of the reasons why I was kind of suppressed, depressed because of the social thing. I went on to Glendale and it wasn't as bad, I was surprised. I thought I was going to have to deal with that again. It was kind of rough in the ninth grade, but as you know everybody matures a little bit and it got better.

However, some parents and siblings, as well as respondents, were particularly disgruntled with the desegregation of Glendale. Chris, older brother of printing student Alex Henley, observed:

> Wakefield [the all-black school] on the west side, why do you need to bring west side town people and bring them over to Glendale. [His mother interjected, "And have buses for them!"] Why don't you just take Charles Street, which runs through the city [north to south], and if you want to go to a vocational school you go to Wakefield and if you're east of Charles Street—you go over here.

Mrs. Henley and her older son also linked her younger son Alex's having to meet a set of unfamiliar entry criteria to efforts to desegregate:

> Here's a kid that had two of the three [criteria], but here's a kid that wanted to go to Glendale because he wanted to take up a trade, he doesn't want to go to college, so why are you telling me I have to send him to Northern [another local high school], yet you'll take these other kids from the other side of town that will come in here and literally do nothing.
>
> Chris: Minorities!

I: What good does it do to have the minorities?

Chris: It looks good.

Alex's father then added:

> They get more money, he [the principal of all-black Wakefield] has
> to have a quota of blacks to have a successful school — I have to have
> so many females and so many Hispanics, I'm not picking an appli-
> ance, if they're black, red, Hispanic — this school says you must have
> so many of them, why? Because the system tells them they've got to
> have that.

White critiques were grounded in long-term histories of association
with Glendale — associations that began during fully segregated eras.
These extensive personal connections to Glendale made the white parents experts compared to black parents on Glendale's strengths and
weaknesses in terms of equipment/facility and curriculum. That exposure helped white students to know which trade fields continued to be
viable within the school and which had fallen into obsolescence. White
parents had monitored the "decline" of Glendale through generations
that sometimes included their parents, but almost invariably included
themselves, peers, siblings, and children, the youngest of whom made up
my sample of 1989 and 1990 graduates. Their knowledge was so detailed
and intimate that several parents were even able to relate what pieces of
remaining machinery had been there during their high school days and
which were supposed to have been replaced over the years.

The Henley family is a case in point. Mr. Henley broke the history of
the school into three significant eras: the one during which he attended
Glendale, a second one that coincided with his two older sons' attendance, and finally the current era, in which the prospects for youngest
son Alex's generation looked grim:

> He [points to his older son Chris, who is sitting at the dining room
> table] got enough training to get him out and get a job. Sean, who is
> two years behind him — he went through the class, he got whatever

experience he learned, whatever he could — he got a job within the trade. Which is why you go to vocational school. Alex went, he went and learned the basics of the trade and where did he go — to the gas station. Now, I ain't knocking the kid for going to a gas station, as long as it works and it puts money in your pocket, that's the name of the game. You go where you can make a buck. How come he had to wait six months [to get his current job as a printer's helper], that's telling me something. That's telling me that what's coming out — there's no jobs.

Up to this point, Mr. Henley had offered a nonracial account of his youngest son's early employment difficulties that rested on the view that the printing industry is changing and that there are fewer good jobs available directly after graduation. From here on, however, Mr. Henley shifted into a discussion that was critical of black administrators and suggested that equipment was being stolen right under their noses. Mr. Henley had visited Glendale on a number of occasions and had confronted one of his former classmates, who currently works within the school system.

I'm standing in this class — this is fifteen years after I get out — where's the machinery? I walk in the building and there's approximately seventy to one hundred thousand dollars worth of equipment at that time, and it's gone. Ben [a current shop teacher and Mr. Henley's former Glendale classmate] says, "It's outdated." I said, "It's outdated, tell you what you do, Ben, get your ass in my car and I'll take you down to where you can see them [pieces of these types of equipment currently in use] — it's outdated!" I'll show you a picture of these machines. This guy goes in and says, "What's that, what's that?"

Mr. Henley identified specific blacks whom he held accountable for Glendale's decline. The following exchange between myself and Mr. Henley illustrates the proprietary relationship of whites to Glendale, including loudly voiced concerns about staff and equipment. First Mr. Henley complains about a district coordinator with no practical trade experience, then he describes a heated confrontation with Glendale's black woman principal.

> I dealt with the coordinator for the city of Baltimore, a nice guy, black fellow — I hate to bring race into it, but it's all a part of it, that's how he got his job and he'll tell you to your face — that's how I got my job — I'm black and I got a college degree. I said, "Let me ask you something, when was the last time you worked in a shop?" Never. Dynamite! [Mr. Henley continues incredulously:] This guy's going to tell me what the hell is going on in industry? You can read all the flunky books you want and you can learn — this guy was a coordinator for industry and education!

> I: *And had never been in industry?*

> Right. I get the director of vocational education [an old classmate] and I said, "Jack get your ass up here" — she [Glendale's black female principal] comes walking in — I told Jack, "She's got fifteen minutes to get her ass here or she can forget this shit!"

> I: *Were you able to work something out with her?*

> . . . Oh, I took her upstairs and said, "Now I'm taking my time and now I want you to take your time" — I said, "You find $100,000 worth of equipment that got stolen out of here." She said, "What do you mean?" I said, "See that switch on the wall, it's a cylindrical grinder, that's a file cabinet — whether you know it or not — under that switch and it ain't connected to shit. That's a radial drill press connection — where the hell is it at? It's gone. Now how do I know it, because I was here and I learned on this shit. Now I want you to tell me why it ain't here! It's because somebody made a fortune. They tell me they ain't used in industry — I can prove that it is used in industry today." And nothing came in after it went out. "Now," I said, "I'm going to give *you* the job, you tell me where the hell it went! Now, let me tell you, if you don't find out where the hell it goes, I'm going to find out, but you ain't going to like what I find out when you hear about it. Let me tell you something, it's called WGEZ, WBAL, I said I'll blow your ship right out of the water and your big salary. And you can tell Schaffer [the governor] that and the rest of the SOBs down there!"

Glendale, as a city school in the all-too-familiar middle stages of desegregation — characterized by decreased funding per pupil, growing numbers of black teachers, administrative staff, and students, but not quite a black majority yet — was two different schools from the point of view of the white and black students and their families. For whites, Glendale was euphemistically becoming "their" — meaning blacks' — school and thus less desirable. For blacks, Glendale was an almost untried, fairly close neighborhood school that was becoming increasingly hospitable. None of the black parents had attended Glendale, and only a few of the black graduates' older siblings had. As an institution, white families had less and less stake in Glendale, while black families did not seem to be aware of Glendale's real or imagined shortcomings. Although both groups seemed to understand changes in Baltimore's job structure that logically reduced the number of available blue-collar job openings, only whites seemed distressed at the transition in course offerings Glendale seemed to be making, which shifted resources away from traditional trades and toward areas like business, food preparation, nursing, and cosmetology — and thereby from a predominantly male to an increasingly female student body.

White Glendale students benefit from being privy to some accurate but not publicly available information about Glendale's changing status. This information is important because it helps white students to make more informed choices about which courses of study and teachers are best, and how to accurately perceive and convey to potential employers Glendale's strengths and weaknesses as an institution. Being able to convey an understanding of the strengths and weaknesses of training experiences to employers could be an important advantage in the interview setting, since urban employers often voice concerns about the preparation of young prospective employees. In addition, the notion that white parents' less positive assessments of Glendale would be shared, perhaps after some delay, by similarly aged white employers in the area hardly requires a leap of faith. That it was having an effect on the school's ability to place black students effectively I will demonstrate.

THE RACIALIZATION OF GLENDALE'S
WORK-STUDY PROGRAM

Two thirds of Glendale students attempt to get into work-study jobs by their junior year. At Glendale, the work-study program is the sole institution-based transition mechanism available to students. As a formal linkage mechanism, it is designed to use meritocratic and semistandardized selection procedures to match students with jobs. It is the closest approximation to an open and free job placement market that Glendale has. But in practice the work-study program is neither highly competitive nor exhaustive. Instead, the program is flexible and accommodating of student initiative. Sometimes students find a summer job, for example, that they successfully convert into an academic work-study. Because students, families, teachers, and employers may initiate the contact that eventually becomes a work-study opportunity, it is impossible to determine whether or in what ways the allocation of work-study jobs is based solely on merit. Flexibility notwithstanding, Glendale's work-study program still relies extensively on local employers who are willing to hire young workers, and so a good deal of work is put into maintaining good relationships with such employers.

Years ago, the process of institutional network maintenance (between schools and local businesses) took place through the day-to-day interactions of school officials and local employers and senior workers. Through these interactions (as well as more formal means), school officials were notified about job openings and employers were notified about promising older students. The relationships that developed between senior workers/employers and teachers, counselors, and administrators were personal as well as professional. Mr. Henley's fairly informal relationships with former classmates (Ben and Jack, mentioned earlier) who now occupy teaching and administrative positions within the public school system provide a contemporary example of the patterns that typified relationships between parents, senior workers, and school officials. These long-term, close personal relationships, which encouraged trust and discouraged malfeasance, helped to facilitate the allocation tasks of schools like Glendale.

Granovetter suggests that these professional/personal overlaps reveal the social embeddedness of institutions, such as schools, and of processes like getting a job. He has shown that what appear to be impersonally or bureaucratically organized economic interactions are both facilitated and discouraged as a part of the normal functioning of sets of extensive overlapping social networks. Indeed, Granovetter characterizes economic action as socially embedded *because* it takes place in the context of and is influenced by personal and social relationships.[1] But twentieth-century patterns of racial segregation — residential, educational, and occupational — have helped create and maintain racially segregated (nonoverlapping) networks among whites and blacks. Thus, Glendale's personnel and student reconfiguration from majority white male toward majority black male and female, not surprisingly, affects institutional ties.

The task of institutional network maintenance between schools and local employers during the time that my respondents were making the school-work transition rested directly with Lydia Williams. A part-time staff member who had been running the work-study program for six years, she was responsible for over three hundred students a year and for maintaining contact with regular employers like Baltimore Gas and Electric, United States Federal Guaranty, the Cannell Corporation, and Hechingers, as well as for seeking out new business contacts. These contacts are a main linkage mechanism connecting Glendale students to jobs in auto mechanics, electrical construction, carpentry, brick masonry, and other trade jobs.

Ms. Williams did not know whether she was the first woman or African-American to serve as the work-study coordinator, but she expressed concerns about how some white employers responded to her and the black students that she had sent to interviews. Her explanation recalls some of the Henleys' observations:

Well, you have to understand that Glendale was all-white for most
of its history — blacks have only come into the administration in
the last few years, and that has not been so easy either. For example,
the former principal and vice principals have been white men,
and they established some of the work-study networks over twenty
years ago. So now, the school is over half black and the principal
is a black woman and the work-study coordinator is black, and
the employers are expecting white people — white students, white
principals. The shop teachers are still white but a lot of the employers are, you see, former students — they graduated years ago when
it was still just "their" school. They don't know what to make of us
now.

Although she did not go into detail, Ms. Williams seemed aware that
many of the jobs that students, especially whites, located for work-study
came not from her office but through former students and white male
teachers who staff the machine and trowel trades, carpentry, auto
mechanics, electronics, and electrical construction shops. When asked
whether they work with her, she laughed somewhat sarcastically, but
then replied very seriously:

They have been here a long time. They are good teachers and they
know their fields, but some were here before Glendale began admit-
ting black students.

I: *Do black male students have difficulties with them?*

I think so, I think that the black males don't feel that they are the
important students in the classrooms where there are also white
male students. Some of the better black students have had some
pretty rough incidents with them. Talk to H. S., if you get a chance.
He was a very good work-study student, but you wouldn't know it
to look at his record.

I: *What do you mean?*

He has a file this long (opens her arms as wide as possible) and he is
one that gets great reports from employers, even the ones I'm not so
sure about.

The lack of networking support from white male teachers and students makes black students more dependent on interviews as a mechanism for placement. Interviews, however, presented additional difficulties for black students. Indeed, these difficulties were not surprising to Ms. Williams, since sometimes white employers would hear *her* voice, become very rude, and quickly get off the phone. These interviewing problems were so discouraging to black students that some seemed willing to work only in settings that were already integrated.

> I have sent several [black] students on interviews where they came back and said, "They took one look at me and it was over." One student said they kept him waiting an hour, then told him that there was no one there who could interview him. Another one said the boss never looked at him after he came in the door. These experiences have been very discouraging. A lot of the black males come into my office acting like they don't want to interview. They say, "Ms. Williams, any blacks there?

I asked Ms. Williams if black students had become more reluctant to go to interviews after hearing other students' negative stories. She responded:

> They [black students] will go, but [if hired] some won't stay long if there are no other blacks at the job. They get sick of the little comments all the time. I talk to them about it, but mostly I just try to send them where it's less likely to happen, or those that are strong I send and they just cope with it. I tell them to take notes on the meeting, you know, the interview, and we go over that and then we wait to hear something. We talk about how it went and I follow up by calling and talking to the person who interviewed them. Sometimes I can tell that I'm never going to hear from that employer again — and this is before a student has even had a chance to screw up! A lot of times, though, it's hard to tell which way it will go. You know, you try to ask a lot of questions to see, but you can never tell till you've actually sent somebody. And then sometimes one person will work out but another one won't, so it's really hard to predict some of them.

After encountering a number of such experiences, Ms. Williams began to engage in employer-screening processes in an attempt to gauge whether certain white employers would be willing and able to desegregate their work places. It was not uncommon for Ms. Williams to use a number of "investigative" strategies, such as "feeling the employer out," examining the address of the business to determine if it was in a traditionally hostile neighborhood, asking among friends what people had heard about the racial dynamics of certain areas or employers, conducting covert inspections by posing as a customer, and asking racially sensitive white work-study students what they thought about certain employers. On occasion, she engaged in some informal testing of racial receptivity by sending a very good black student and a white student on interviews with employers she suspected might be prejudiced. The outcomes of these attempts have varied, but once both were hired. In that case, the power of race was manifest. She continued:

> I found out later that the white student had been asked about the black student. You know, what's he like, can he do the work? Luckily, the white student admitted that the black student was the best student in the class.

I: Do you think this happens often?

What? You mean white students being asked about black students? No, not really, I just think that the white males are assumed to be tight [well-prepared] and the black males are assumed to be potential problems.

Ms. Williams, though socially active in the black community, had little personal contact with white employers beyond telephone calls made from her office. Her efforts were in part designed to prevent black students from having discouraging early experiences that might dampen their self-confidence as young workers, but a second reason for her screening activities was to maintain contacts that had been established before she took on the work-study coordinator position.

Since many vocationally trained students hope to get jobs close to their homes, the views of local employers, especially those whose job openings are a necessary component of the formal work-study program, are extremely important. Because of the ties that develop over time between schools and local employers, job placement counselors like Ms. Williams put a great deal of work into creating new employer leads, maintaining satisfaction among current work-study employers, and troubleshooting in view of matching the "right" sorts of students to available job openings. One way she attempts to keep connections alive is by accommodating some of the employers' preferences for white students. She has also developed a careful screening process in her efforts to successfully connect black students to mainly white employers. Regarding students, she explained: "That's why we work so hard to make sure that the students we send are ready. We practice interviews, I give the black students hard questions to answer, oh, I coach them on lots of questions and answers. By the time I send them out they are ready, but lots of them are scared." She continued, "After I advertise the positions and the students begin to come in, I'm very particular — I mean *very* particular. I look for attendance, punctuality, a B average at least. For some of the students, grades cannot get them in the jobs they really want. See, a majority of the students don't have the licensing the jobs require, like in the mechanics field." In the same breath, Ms. Williams mentioned a nonmerit-based obstacle that affected black students: "And how they will get there. Transportation is very important. Making sure they can get to the job is a real issue. Sometimes I have to take them myself. I have called some students to make sure they get up on time, but mostly I drop them off near work or near a bus stop that will get them to the job." While it may be that white students who needed transportation chose not to ask Ms. Williams, she has never had to take a white student to a place of employment. It is likely, given my finding that a substantial number of white students already had cars before they graduated from Glendale, that transportation, whether to jobs outside or within the city, was a bigger obstacle for black students than for white students. It's also likely that some white students would not want or need a black person to enter their neighborhood to do them a favor.

Lydia Williams pointed out many issues that I had not anticipated when I began the study. For example, although I had known that Glendale was originally an all-white school, I had not anticipated that some of the work-study employers would be former graduates who would expect students similar to themselves to be sent for interviews. In addition, Lydia Williams' efforts to gauge employer preferences and tolerance levels provides a glimpse of what the black males in the study must have done for interviews — with little help once they left school. Finally, alongside the formal transition system — largely the work-study and job placement coordination efforts of Ms. Williams — is an informal transition system run by white male teachers that was utilized extensively by white males but very infrequently by black males in this study.

MAKING IT PERSONAL: WHITE MALE TEACHERS AND GLENDALE'S INFORMAL WORK-STUDY PROGRAM

In the course of interviewing, I was struck by the number of white male students whose first training-related jobs were not initiated through the work-study office listings, but rather through the efforts of white male trade teachers. These teachers arranged both regular and "off-the-books" or "side" jobs for white male students — frequently in their own small businesses. Although similar numbers of white and black students took courses with white male teachers, only white students were provided significant trade-related jobs with the teachers themselves, and only white students were helped specifically through the personal contacts of the teachers. Black males received help from white teachers far less frequently, and usually such help was formalized and connected to school-based programs, such as the Commonwealth Plus program or the work-study office run by Ms. Williams. After hearing a number of students describe their work transition experiences, I determined that Glendale had both a formal work-study program that provided information and assistance to the entire student body, and an informal work-study program run by white male teachers that provided jobs and job leads only to selected students — in the case of my sample, white male students.

For white students, teacher assistance provided a key transition mechanism into stable employment. Several subpatterns were evident. In the first pattern, a number of students remained in jobs that teachers helped them get while in school. By the time of the interviews, these students had begun to build seniority and were taking advantage of a full set of employment benefits and receiving additional training at their company's expense. Others, pursuing the second pattern of assistance from teachers, used their early earnings to purchase cars and tools that made it possible for them to run their own side businesses, usually while they continued to work for others. In the third pattern, a small minority of the white male students had not received significant help from a white male teacher. Regardless of their transition pattern, nearly all of the white students had no (or only brief) periods of unemployment, even though many had switched jobs a number of times.

In this section, I focus mainly on teacher-assisted transitions. Wherever possible, I compare the experiences of black and white students within the same trades. In certain trade areas, there were no comparable blacks and whites. For each trade, I provide representative cases to show important differences in the racial patterns. I also indicate what category of success the students experienced: High Success Within Field (HSW), High Success Outside Field (HSO), Moderate Success Within or Outside Field (MSW/O), Low Success (LS), or Miscellaneous (MISC).

Students Who Studied Brick Masonry with Mr. Spano

Four of the students in my sample, two black and two white, studied brick masonry with Tim Spano, who had taught at Glendale for many years. All four saw Mr. Spano as a very friendly and competent teacher who offered help in the job search. Mr. Spano's reputation as a caring instructor seemed well earned, since he was mentioned even by students outside of his trade area as one of the most helpful teachers at Glendale. But, despite Mr. Spano's popularity with both black and white students, there were important differences in his assistance efforts on behalf of the black and white men in this study.

Jermaine Decker (MSO), a black student who currently works as a truck driver for a produce company, has never had a formal job laying brick. Nevertheless, Jermaine felt very supported by Mr. Spano: "He noticed I was good and he said we'll send you to some companies and to VICA [a state-wide trade competition open to vocational students] to show you are capable of doing the job well." Even though VICA did not turn out so well—Jermaine lost badly in the competition—Jermaine attempted to find a work-study job in his junior year without Mr. Spano's help. Ultimately, Jermaine did not get a work-study job; instead his only brick work for pay has been on infrequent side jobs with his father in their neighborhood.

Another black student, Allen Howard (MSO), listed Mr. Spano as someone who had offered to write letters of recommendation, make phone calls, or serve as a reference if necessary. When I asked if he'd gotten a job as a result of Mr. Spano's help, Allen replied,

> Well, I ain't never really put his name down, he always said I could use his name if I wanted him for a reference, just to help me out to get a job or anything like that.
>
> I: *He extended his hand to, like, put in a word for you, but you didn't follow up on that job, or . . . ?*
>
> He never really set up no jobs or nothing like that but he said if he knew somebody that needed some people he would recommend me.

Allen currently works as a delivery truck driver. Allen thus received verbal support and encouragement from Mr. Spano, but not active material assistance. I asked him if he felt that his education at Glendale was sufficient to get him the kind of job he'd had in mind. Interestingly, in his answer, Allen focused less on brick mason skills than on interview etiquette. Since Allen seemed unable to get stable employment within his trade, I asked if he'd talked to anyone, like a teacher, about getting a job. He replied with resignation, "I have, a couple of times when I was unemployed, say like — I was just — I put everything in God's hands and let him take care of it." Both Jermaine and Allen earned Bs and Cs in their coursework with Mr. Spano, and both had solid attendance records. Their situations stand in contrast to those of white students Mr. Spano taught.

Jeff Packer (HSO), who is currently a stock clerk with a large warehouse-style department store, was one of Mr. Spano's white students. While in high school, Jeff got two work-study jobs and a good number of side jobs laying brick. He got his first work-study job on his own because, as he explained, "I knew the guy, Bill Huston, who owned the company [B & J Construction], that was on Webster Street [near his home]." Mr. Spano got him his work-study permit. Spano also helped with his second work-study, during his senior year. Jeff explained how he got a job with L & K Tile Company: "He came to our school — his name was Lee Kawicki — or something like that — he was the owner. He was looking for help. I started off as a laborer and then went up the trade. We did ceramic tile, marble, basically anything I've done on floors." When I asked Jeff about which instructor helped him the most, he again spoke of Mr. Spano.

> Spano — he was more of a friend to everybody than a teacher, he'd help us with other teachers, like if we got into trouble, he'd go find out what was the trouble.

I: Did any of your instructors offer to write letters for you . . .

Yes, they would. He'd [Spano] find us jobs, whatever we wanted. If we were willing to find jobs, he'd find us a place to work, if we wanted to work.

I: Did you get a job as a result of this kind of help?

Yes, the tile job, and then he gave me a lot of side jobs.

I: Did you work with him sometimes?

Yes, I worked with him too. When I was in high school, I knew I
wanted to go in the service, I also knew I wanted to be a cop. Spano
said he could get me a job as an apprentice in masonry, like a couple
of my friends did [friend Tom Smith is mentioned].

Jeff, modeling Mr. Spano's and others' networking practices, currently
does side jobs where he hires a number of people to assist him. He
explained that it was possible to do side jobs because he had all the necessary tools, which he'd bought while still in high school. Jeff had
amassed what he estimated was close to eight thousand dollars worth of
tools from working side jobs and knowing where to purchase them cheap.
He explained why these jobs were so lucrative and how he had access to
them.

It was unlimited really if you had enough people to work in the
construction field, but you never had people. . . . What I was making
on a side job, if I knew I could have a side job every week I'd say
maybe forty thousand dollars just myself. In my senior year I hired
out Tom Smith, we did a job right off the Hartford Road, a porch-
like patio thing, just resetting the brick — I made, for just three of
us at work I made like a thousand dollars and I had my brother as a
laborer and he made a couple of hundred and Tom made like three
hundred. I did all the calling around and got all the concrete trucks
and all.

Jeff still imagines, even when he becomes a police officer, that he can do
ceramic masonry as a sideline.

Later in the interview, Jeff described how a retired Glendale teacher
helped him and other white students get side and formal jobs during his
senior year.

Then I also did some teacher's house down in Cambridge — for
Mr. Wilson — I think he retired. I did all his ceramic tile. He put
in a brand new house right on the water, so everything had to be
ceramic tile, every room — and he had a big home.

I: *How much did you make?*

For him I did it by the hour seven dollars, plus gas and he let me stay at the house and he fed us. There were a couple of us down there. He had some guy worked up in the wood shop [carpentry] area that helped us with the woodwork. So that was okay, we did it more as a friend than . . . [his voice trails off].

In comparison to his effective utilization of personal networks, Jeff made little use of the formal transition mechanisms. He never met with Lydia Williams, viewing her office as an unnecessary bureaucratic inconvenience for students like himself. "I guess the only person I ever got help from was Spano. The counselors had addresses and stuff, but they were so far outdated — the list they had of construction companies, half of them would be open one day and closed the next. They didn't update the lists periodically." Jeff estimated that he had had two formal jobs related to his training but lots of informal ones, "Since I've graduated I've had maybe ten jobs, but while I was in school, every weekend seemed like I had a new job."

Danny O'Brien (HSO), another white student who currently installs residential and commercial burglar alarms and lays brick on the side, relayed experiences similar to Jeff's. Danny mentioned a job with a local construction company, started by a graduate of Glendale, which became a work-study that Mr. Spano helped him to get. I probed, "He recommended you for the work-study position and you already knew the guy who owned the company?" "No, I'd never met my boss," Danny replied. I continued, "So Sandon [the owner] was one of his [Mr. Spano's] students probably?" Danny answered, "Right."

I asked Danny about the number of jobs that he'd done with Mr. Spano. He mentioned five specific jobs, more than one of them subsequent to graduating.

I: Did he just give you a call and say I've got a job, even though you'd already graduated? Did he also use guys who were in the current class?

Yes. [Danny then mentioned three of his classmates who'd recently worked with Mr. Spano; all three were white.]

I asked Danny how many jobs he'd had related to his training in masonry. First, he mentioned having done a few side jobs that involved putting up fences, but he continued, "I do a lot of side jobs with brick too. . . . I've probably done thirty or thirty-five side jobs [laying brick or tiles]. I then asked Danny if he had met with Ms. Williams to arrange his work-study jobs; he replied, "No, I've heard of her, but I never met her." He answered similarly when I asked if any of his teachers, counselors, or principals had suggested that he take any training beyond high school. He replied, "No, I never spoke to my principals. I didn't even know their names."

Mr. Spano's help went beyond masonry students. Danny suggested that an electrical construction student, Josh Schacter (HSW), was good friends with Mr. Spano. Josh, a white student who was working for his brothers' construction firm when I interviewed him, received extensive help from a couple of his teachers early in the transition process. Josh had been working side jobs for teachers as early as the tenth grade. He recalled a number of side jobs he did while working part-time at Memorial Stadium with the Orioles organization: on weekends, during the season, he worked as a brick mason's tender, earning eighty dollars a day. The density of Josh's network became apparent when I asked him how he got one of his first jobs. Josh explained:

From school, the brick mason was the bricklaying teacher at school.

I: Which teacher?

Tim Spano, he taught my brother, he worked for him too. All my brothers.

I: How many brothers?

Four.

Another teacher helped Josh to change jobs so that he could leave a company where he was unhappy. He left with his next job already in hand.

I: How did you get this job?

I was notified by my old teacher, Jack Dodd; his son works there.

I: How did he notify you, did he give you a call?

Yes, I called him and asked him about the company because he told me his son worked there.

I: What did he say?

He said there was a position open at entry level, for a commercial electrician.

Josh mentioned Mr. Dodd as one of ten persons he felt close enough to contact if he needed help getting another job. I asked how he would get in touch with those people. Josh explained:

Right now it would be kind of shaky but if I really had to I could go back to school and through them or something like that.

I: What do you mean?

Through Mr. Dodd, he had a lot of connections.

Students Who Studied Electrical Construction with Mr. Hinkel and Mr. Dodd

Of all of the trade fields offered at Glendale, the most prestigious is electrical construction. If young men could find jobs in the construction trades — a stable and growing sector in Baltimore's economy — they could make wages comparable to those of some professional and managerial workers. Thus what happens between electrical construction teachers and students has a big impact on the school-to-work transition. While all of the electrical construction students I interviewed respected Mr. Hinkel and Mr. Dodd, black males had been unable to establish close relationships with either teacher, had frequently had memorable altercations with one or both teachers, and had received only occasional assistance from them. Of the two black students who got minor assistance from the teachers, only one student attained a job as a result of that help, and it was a short-lived one. The contrast with the white men's experiences with these teachers is striking: indeed, only one white male got minor assistance, most saying that they were helped extensively. Unlike the white students (including those outside of the trade, like Josh Schacter), who saw these teachers as personal friends, black students seemed to feel that their relationship with these teachers remained within the context of formal student-teacher roles. More disturbingly, two of the black students worried about Mr. Hinkel's racial attitudes, while Mr. Dodd's racial record was widely debated. Because of racial concerns, some black students were reluctant to seek help from these teachers.

At least partly because of the employment success I found among the white students who studied with Mr. Hinkel and Mr. Dodd, I wanted to be sure that I could locate and interview some of the black students who seemed highly competent in the electrical construction trade. I asked all of the electrical construction students for the names of the best black students. Ron Curtis was one of the first white students to mention Hank Searles, the student Ms. Williams had insisted I interview:

> In my class, Hank Searles — he was a good guy, he ranked right
> up there with me and Josh, he got a work-study job, he worked
> for Miles Electric and he's one of the ones that told me it wasn't
> that great [a family-owned firm that tended to promote family first].
> He worked in the eleventh-grade shop for a short time, two months,
> and then he got his work-study job and he was out! And he was out
> the entire senior year too. I would say he was the top black student.

Hank Searles (HSW) is the only black student who could be considered highly successful within his trade at the time I conducted the interviews for this study. I found Hank extremely personable in the interview, even though, as Ms. Williams indicated, he had a lengthy file of disturbing in-school incidents with some white male teachers. In the interview, I paid even more attention than usual to his deportment, looking for indications of arrogance, hostility, or other characteristics that urban employers sometimes associate with young black male workers. I detected none.

Hank's negative experiences with white male teachers are all the more difficult to understand because he was also the only black student (by the time of my interviews) who had established lasting relationships with any white tradesmen. I'll discuss these relationships in detail later. Importantly, none of these trade relationships were with school personnel or sustained through them. Unlike other black students, Hank was able to use his ties to this employer network to provide access for other blacks. He observed at one point, almost as an afterthought, "I got Michael a job at Fleet Electric — I forgot about that."

Hank's description of his relationships with his trade teachers is complex, even contradictory in some ways. For example, when I asked Hank which teacher helped him the most, he said Mr. Hinkel. But later, when I followed up with "Did you like Mr. Hinkel a lot?" Hank replied, "No, I couldn't stand him, but he helped me a lot. I listened to him. He was a good teacher, but he had an attitude problem. [I: A racial attitude problem?] I think so."

He also described difficulties he'd had with Mr. Dodd when I asked him, "How did you feel about these men?"

> Mr. Hinkel was a good teacher, Mr. Skene [retired], I liked him a lot — we used to sit around and joke. Mr. Dodd, I only knew him for a little while, because I had come off of work-study and was in his class for a couple of months. He respected me because he knew I could do the work real well so he moved me along as quickly as he could to get me to catch up, but me and him had problems with small stuff. What happened was, we had a new rule come into effect with the way we could dress in school. And one day we couldn't wear "Used Jeans" [a popular brand of jeans associated with hip-hop style] because there were tears in them, no cotton T-shirts with no collar, no sweatsuits, but you could wear the sweatshirt. He tried to say that I couldn't wear the sweatshirt one day and we got into [it] one day and from then on we rarely had too much to say to each other. He was the teacher and I was the student and we kept it like that.

At another point,, though, Hank made clear that Mr. Dodd exerted an effort on behalf of other black students, including Michael Breen, Dante Dobbins, and Montel Shire. Hank explained,

> All three of them guys got jobs at electrical companies and Mr. Dodd helped. . . . He [Mr. Dodd] was a good teacher too. I'm not going to say nothing's wrong with him. He even got a few guys and me jobs, but when those jobs came up, I was probably the most qualified for one of them jobs, but he gave one of the other guys a chance to get on work-study because I had already been on it. We still was on that teacher-student relationship.

Despite Hank's concessions that Mr. Hinkel and Mr. Dodd were good teachers, little trust developed between Hank and either teacher. Hank suggested that Mr. Dodd might have been reluctant to write a letter of recommendation for him, even though he felt that Mr. Dodd respected his work. When I asked if Mr. Hinkel had ever written a letter for him or if he'd ever asked him to, he replied,

> No, I never asked him.

> *I: Would he [have written one] if you had asked him?*

> Yes, but I don't think I would have asked him because I think he had a touch of prejudice.

Hank's relationships with Mr. Hinkel and Mr. Dodd never assumed the tone or content of the friendship-based relationships that developed between the teachers and Josh Schacter and Ron Curtis. Instead, Hank became close to Ms. Williams: "I had to go through Lydia Williams, but I found the job myself and then told Ms. Williams about all of that. We [he and his wife] still talk to Ms. Williams all the time, we see her a lot. My wife talks to her a lot, my wife graduated from Glendale too." The centrality of Ms. Williams' assistance came up again when I asked Hank, "Would you say you were satisfied with the assistance you received from instructors, counselors, or other school personnel in your job search?"

He replied, "Very satisfied: Miss Williams did a good job, she always helped you out."

I interviewed other electrical construction students, three of whom were black students who had not gotten assistance from Mr. Dodd or Mr. Hinkel. One of the students, Craig Mourning (LS), was mentioned by both Hank Searles and one of the white electrical construction students as being pretty strong in the trade. At the time of the interviews, Craig had not yet gotten a job in the construction trade and had begun to consider entering the ministry. While he was in high school, he had also expressed an interest in the rap music business. Like Hank, Craig respected the trade teachers but had some difficult interactions with them. I asked Craig if other students had warned him about certain instructors, and he mentioned Mr. Hinkel, who he said had a reputation for being strict. I asked if the students respected Mr. Hinkel. Craig replied,

> Yes, I would say so. To an extent, I think they respected him because he knew his work. A lot of his ways I don't think they respected because personally he showed, he sort of showed favoritism.

> I: *Toward whom?*

> We had two white guys in the class — Josh Schacter and Ron Curtis — both of these are cool guys, both of them was cool. But Mr. Hinkel sort of put them on a pedestal that I don't think was fair. It was always Ron and Schacter, Ron and Schacter this and that.

> I: *Did they get recommended for work-study?*

> I think so. Josh already had a job with Milton Electric. Now Rob, he helped Mr. Hinkel on things on weekends if I'm not mistaken.

> I: *Did Mr. Hinkel ever invite black males to help him, do you know?*

> He did, but not in our class. The thing that's funny about that is the best guy in the class was black, a guy named Hank Searles.

Craig initially described a somewhat better relationship with Mr. Dodd than with Mr. Hinkel. When I asked if any instructors had offered to write recommendation letters, serve as references, or make phone calls to employers, Craig explained:

> No, but Mr. Dodd had a lot of confidence in me. He told me that I could have been the best in the class, he saw that in me and he felt that I could become a great electrician or I could be anything really if I applied myself. But he really convinced himself of it. If I would have pursued that and I hadn't lost interest, then he probably would have [provided] me with a reference.

I: Could he have recommended you for a work-study?

> I could have been on work-study, I could have been on work-study at B,G and E in eleventh grade, but they said that no one in the class had the attendance, everyone had missed too many days is what he was saying. Personally myself, I think they were a little bit too harsh, because I had a 97 percent attendance [he is a Commonwealth Plus — solid grades and attendance — student] throughout the year. Out of 180 days, I missed, like four days. My ninth grade year and my tenth grade year, in my eleventh grade year — by the time they got to me, I had missed maybe five or six, but that wasn't enough for them. They expected people to miss like one day in ten years. I can understand they want people to have good attendance, but I mean, be real, that's asking a little too much.

Craig mentioned Mr. Dodd again when I asked if he'd ever encountered any trouble with instructors that might have made them unlikely to recommend him for specific jobs or as a work-study candidate. Craig was very vague in his description of the problem, but it seemed to relate to a school incident and to Mr. Dodd's opinions about his pursuing rap music. In one instance, Craig recalled Mr. Dodd disapproving of his reaction to having to replace a combination lock that had been stolen from his locker. Craig was dependent upon his grandparents and did not like to ask them for money. He expected the school to replace the stolen lock. He indicated that Mr. Dodd felt he had overreacted to the problem. Mr. Dodd also seemed frustrated with him because he planned to pursue rap music. Craig explained that he had gravitated to music by his senior year: "Yes, by twelfth grade, I knew that's what I wanted to be and he [Mr. Dodd] knew that and I don't think he appreciated it. So when I came up to him about certain things, he was like, he's not going to pursue this anyway, so it doesn't matter as much." But before Craig mentioned his change in interest, he described the difficulties he faced as a result of not having a car or the appropriate tools for work.

> If I had pursued it [work as an electrician], then I would have had to get a license, and I would have had to go out and get my own tools, which is money I didn't have. . . . Graduating from high school, you don't have any money. . . . Most of the people that have it either have parents that have the money to get it for them or they got money while they was in school. When I was in school, I had a tool belt and I had a couple of tools, but they were cheap tools. It was enough to get my work done in school, but not on the job. They'd be like, "You can't use that, you need to get. . . . While you're in school, if you don't have your own personal tools, they had tools for you to use in school. But when you leave the school, the tool stays.

Craig commented, a few times during the interview, on the relationships he observed between Hank Searles and the two shop teachers. At times, Craig seemed to be talking only about Hank; at other times he used the pronoun "we." I asked Craig, "Personally, do you think Hank could have gotten more help?"

> Yes, I know he could have because he was the best in class. The only reason that I don't think that he didn't get as much help as he could have as far as finding employment is concerned — he did have things holding him back, he didn't have the best attendance in the world, but he was the best in the class. He finished his work before everybody, he was doing things toward the end of the year that nobody else was even doing. When he got out, he got to go to work-study. The place that he was [when he left the class to do work-study], some people still didn't even reach during the whole year. He was fast, and it's not like he was necessarily rushing, he was good. [Then he shifts to the collective.] Mr. Hinkel, I don't think cared for us too much.

I: Do you think it was racial, or attitude, or do you think it was a combination?

I think it was personal because Hank didn't particularly — Mr. Hinkel was all right, but they didn't get along too well because a lot of things happened Searles was blamed for and I don't think he appreciated it.

Hank came up at another time during the interview, when I asked if teachers would have given references or a call for anyone in the class: "No. Hank didn't really get along with Mr. Hinkel or Mr. Dodd. . . . Because he didn't do things the way they wanted him to basically is what I think; he knew the work. He does have sort of a temper, but when you . . . when teachers treat you a certain way, that's only natural." In elaborating on how Searles was treated, Craig recalled an incident that occurred while Hank was on work-study:

Searles just happened to come in the classroom because he didn't go to work that day or, whatever the case is, it was like, all right Joe, pay attention, do this and do that, and he could be paying attention but maybe not. He [Mr. Dodd] would call on Searles for a question, and he could answer the question but it might not have been the way he wanted him to answer the question — you know. The boy knew the work, he was good, but I don't think his style for the way of doing things was the way that they wanted it to be. A lot of times when people teach you how to do things, they expect for you to do it their way instead of developing your own style and I don't think his style was the way they wanted it to be.

I: You're talking about his personal style, the way he handled himself in class? Did he roll his eyes and sit back like this, like, "I don't believe this guy?"

He didn't want to be there, he wanted to be at work.

I: Could everybody tell that?

Everybody knew. A lot of people would have preferred to be at work as opposed to being in the classroom, but it's like, because he got the job and I don't think nobody helped him get the job — I think him and Tyrone [another black student] went out and got the job on their own.

I asked Craig if he was satisfied with the assistance he received from instructors, counselors, or other school personnel. Like Hank, Craig did not voluntarily mention his shop teachers. Instead he mentioned a black woman who ran the Commonwealth Plus program.

> The only person really from a job standpoint that was helping?
> Ms. Morgan, she was the Commonwealth Plus director. . . . She
> told me about several different jobs, I can't call them right off hand.
> One thing I remember was working in a mail room someplace
> downtown. She sent me, and she sent another guy.

However, she was unable to arrange jobs in the trades. Craig remarked that only teachers handled these positions. He recalled that the electrical shop teacher, Don Richards, required students to bring to class the employment section from the Sunday paper. But Craig fully appreciated the other contingencies he would face before being able to secure a job: "Now I can honestly say, there's always people looking for electricians and electrician helpers, it's always in the paper. I've always seen several different jobs for that. But they always require tools, transportation, or they say 'requires tools, experience needed,' there's always experience though, you always need experience." Craig worried that a lack of experience would remain a serious hindrance for him:

> It's like you're persuading them that you can do the work, you can
> tell them that "I worked when I was in school, I put stuff together —
> I've done electrical work," but they want somebody who's been
> experienced in the field, that's actually been out there because they
> can always say, "Well, I'm pretty sure you did things in your school,
> but it's not the same in the real world."

Another black student, Junior Rivers (HSO), who currently delivers sodas and sets up displays for Pepsi, said that he'd gotten a work-study job as a result of help from a Commonwealth Plus director and Mr. Dodd. He was one of five electrical students sent for an interview at Coffman Carpenters. He was somewhat surprised when he got the job, but he only stayed for a couple of months. I asked Junior how it went and he explained, "I didn't like working for Coffman Carpenters at all, they had me doing the shitty job stuff. I was the youngest guy in the company and I was the only black guy in the company, so I was treated different." I asked Junior if it was his age or race that mattered most:

> It was both. For instance, when I would come in to work, when I was on work-study, my first job was to go around and empty — my job title was the same as everybody's and I did the same work as everybody did — and my first job when I came into work was to empty everybody's trash can.

> I: *Who was doing it before you got there?*

> They had to empty their own trash can. That's before I could start my work, before I could set up my work bench, I had to empty everybody's trash can. I didn't mind it.

> I: *Did you ask them why?*

> No, I figured as long as I was getting paid for it, I would go ahead and do it, it wasn't no big thing. It was inside that I was pissed off. . . . Nobody ever got smart with me about it, it's just I felt, "Why do I have to do this?"

Later I asked Junior why he left Coffman's. He said without elaborating, "I left Coffman's cause I got mad."

Black students who studied electrical construction, like Junior, Craig, and Hank, attempted to gain access to the construction labor market with only minimal help, if any, from their shop teachers; frequently the only help was encouragement. Yet, according to the black men, the shop teachers did occasionally provide more active assistance to other black students. However, it is striking how frequently the teachers provided extensive help to white students, many of whom already had numerous family members, neighbors, and friends helping them.

White electrical construction students got considerably more active assistance from the shop teachers, especially Mr. Dodd. I located Ron Curtis, who'd been Josh Schacter's partner for class projects. His experiences much mirrored Josh Schacter's and other white students. Ron (HSW) currently works at Baltimore Gas and Electric. Although he received employment assistance from friends and teachers, all of the jobs within his field, including his current one, came as a result of Mr. Dodd's assistance. Indeed, in his third one, he worked directly for Mr. Dodd. Yet Ron described how Mr. Hinkel, the other electrical construction teacher, paved the way for him to work for the J. Dodd Heating and Air Conditioning Service during his junior summer:

> I had Mr. Hinkel, and he told me Mr. Dodd usually will hire one guy from the eleventh- or twelfth-grade class for a summer job. He had Doug Johnson working for him. He took another job with another electric company and couldn't work for Mr. Dodd anymore, and I was glad to take the job.
>
> *I: Did Mr. Hinkel recommend you to Mr. Dodd?*
>
> I think so.

This summer job (not a work-study), which actually started the spring before school ended, paid $4.00 an hour until school was over and then it went up to $5.00 an hour. Although not as lucrative as some jobs, Ron gained a lot of experience and confidence:

> I learned basically the ins and outs of every air conditioner on the market, so I could tear one apart and fix it and put it back together. We did some central air service; we learned a lot about that. . . . We spent half the time with the air conditioning service and half the time building his house. So that was really an experience. From tearing the house down — I was helping him do that — to pouring the concrete foundation, gutting the house.

On taking a class with him during his senior year, Ron remarked, "We kept it as a teacher-student relationship in the classroom. It was more like friends outside, but he didn't treat me any better than anybody. I was one of the class."

Ron went on to tell me about his first official work-study job, a construction job arranged by Mr. Dodd with electrical contractor Figueroa and Associates. He also mentioned a job with North American Electric that he and Josh Schacter had interviewed for, but that neither got.

> I: *Why didn't you get it?*

> I guess there was no openings at the time. Mr. Dodd's stepson worked there, and he told Mr. Dodd there were some openings and me and Josh should apply, and we did. We filled it out, we were in twelfth grade, we just never heard anything from them. They took our applications and said we'll call you and that was it.

Again, Mr. Dodd was helpful in initiating the interview process through extending an important contact in his own network portfolio to these students. Later, thanks to Mr. Dodd's earlier assistance, Josh began working for this same company.

I asked if Mr. Dodd or Mr. Hinkel had provided recommendation letters for Ron or his partner, Josh Schacter, while they were in the process of finding jobs. Ron said, "I cannot remember if we had letters for that or not. I know I got a letter for B, G & E [his current job]."

Although Ron couldn't find a copy of his letter, another of Mr. Dodd's white students, Sean Mullino, had gotten a letter and provided me with a copy. In Sean's letter, Mr. Dodd certified that Sean had mastered a number of important electrical tasks, such as "installing lighting and power circuits using Romex, armored cable, rigid conduit, and electrical metallic tubing." In addition, Mr. Dodd suggested that Sean had gained valuable work experience while conducting electrical maintenance on the school building. The letter ended:

> Sean is an excellent student who has excelled in every phase of this course. He has an excellent attendance record and can always be trusted to work with minimum supervision.
>
> I feel given the opportunity Sean will make an excellent employee in an electrically related position.

(At the time of my interview, Sean was pursuing a rock music career and doing off-the-books construction jobs on the side. Sean was not a Commonwealth Plus high-attendance student, but Mr. Dodd didn't seem to mind *his* interest in music, unlike that of his black peer, Craig, who was pursuing rap music.)

White Students in Nonoverlapping Fields

In some fields, like machine shop, carpentry, and food services, I was unable to locate both black and white students; this precluded black-white comparisons. In these nonoverlapping fields, the friendship-based relationship patterns between white students and white teachers seemed about as significant as in the other fields. Three cases, machine shop student Darren Zeskind and drafting students Micky Allen and Jermaine Decker, provide illustrative examples.

Darren Zeskind (HSW) is a white machine shop graduate who started work-study in the tenth grade, a year earlier than students are usually allowed to begin work-study jobs. For Darren, it seemed natural to study machine shop, since various family members were machinists. He explained,

> My uncles are all machinists — or have worked in that field at some
> time in their life. . . . I've got two uncles who work down at Bethle-
> hem Steel, I have two cousins — one works at Martin's — another
> who works at the Domino Sugar machine shop — my mother's
> brother, he used to work at Martins . . . and I have another uncle
> who works down on the point [Sparrow's Point] — Bethlehem Steel.

At the time of our interview, Darren had been stably employed for five years and had advanced from minor duties on the shop floor to machinist/journeyman. His main duties were to write and execute programs for the company's computerized numerical control (CNC) lathe. He explained the significance of his age and responsibilities to me: "There are people who . . . don't learn what I do until they're probably twenty-eight or twenty-nine . . . and most places don't have the CNC machines, so people don't get a chance to learn." I asked Darren how he got the job, and he explained that Mr. Wooten, his shop teacher, told him to go down to the shop and apply. Mr. Wooten thought the job would be a good opportunity because it had an in-house apprenticeship program.

Although Mr. Wooten helped Darren, Darren perceived himself as primarily responsible for his own success. According to Darren, "He [Mr. Wooten] just told me where it was and told me to run down there and tell my boss where I was from because I think Mr. Wooten used to work with my boss a long time ago." Darren did, however, credit Mr. Wooten with making it possible for him to start working so early: "He's the one that got me out on work-study in the tenth grade. At Glendale, they would never let you out on work-study in the tenth grade, it had to be eleventh, so Mr. Wooten let me leave school early from his class and not say anything." I asked Darren if he'd spoken with Lydia Williams during this time. He replied, "Yes. She was my counselor, I think. She's the one who I had to fill out some papers, some release forms, have my boss sign them, and then take them back to her. I think we did that in eleventh grade."

Even though Darren and Mr. Wooten did not seem as personally close as some of the other white students and their teachers — Darren was somewhat critical of Mr. Wooten in the interview and never said they were friends — Mr. Wooten made private arrangements for Darren that the school would not have permitted. Thus Darren was the beneficiary of an informal work-study created by a white male teacher.

Another white student got one of his early jobs from a substitute teacher. Drafting student Micky Allen (HSO) got most of his job search assistance from friends, family, and neighbors, but in one instance a teacher helped. He explained:

> There's a teacher at Glendale who had a home improvement company, and I also worked for him part-time. . . . He was a substitute teacher. Mr. Haus, he had an improvement company and needed help part-time after school.
>
> I: *What kinds of things did you do?*
>
> Knock down walls, take out old cabinets. They'd knock down drywall, so we'd have to clean the mess up.

Although this job was only part-time and temporary, the money Micky saved from such jobs enabled him to buy his first car early. By the time of the interview, he was on his third car.

Another white drafting student, Justin Guess (MISC), got help from the drafting teacher while in the eleventh grade. Mr. Gaither helped Justin to get a work-study job in drafting at Purdum and Jeshke, where he stayed through his junior and senior years. Justin told me about the experience: "When I first went there, I did graph work and corrections on drawings, and then I got into starting designing my own CPs. Conduit system layouts. They have a plan and profile and what is . . . they have the manholes in the street and your telephone wire going underground. It was all that sort of thing." Justin eventually left and began pursing an associate's degree in criminal justice because work had become slow at the company and he was only able to get part-time hours. He said that only two months before the interview, he stopped by the firm and they expressed an interest in rehiring him.

Black Students in Nonoverlapping Fields

Black students in trade fields, such as printing and auto mechanics, got assistance from white male teachers more often than black students in electronics or electrical construction. However, there were again differences in the nature of the assistance that was offered. For example, black males were generally supported through formal work-study — Ms. Williams would come to class with job listings — while white males tended to be assisted through teacher initiative and through their personal contacts. Additionally, at the time of the interviews, white males were far more likely than black males to have stayed with companies that had offered them work-study jobs or in side jobs that white male teachers had gotten them.

No black male had stayed beyond a few months in a job that a white teacher helped him get. Like Junior Rivers' experience described earlier, Carlton Fields's experience typifies the rare instances when black males got work-study at least partially through white male teachers. There is considerable confusion over whether the work-study went poorly as a result of racial prejudice among white coworkers or as a result of horse-play among Carlton and two of his friends, who were sent to the job together. After noticing other students getting jobs, Carlton had asked Mr. Lasik for assistance. Mr. Lasik recommended him, helping him and two of his friends, Allen and Jonah, get jobs in a cabinet-making firm. None of the three stayed at the plant long, becoming frustrated with the menial tasks, low pay, and racial politics:

> They told us, "You don't know anything, so we're going to have to tell you everything." So, we were basically like helpers. . . . They didn't let us do a lot of things we wanted to do, they didn't have much work to do, so we ended up sweeping floors, we didn't have a job [actually working on cabinets]. We had to work — we were assigned to a person and . . . they were telling us what to do and we would help them and most of the time they were very limited in the things they knew how to do also.

Initially, Carlton reported that working in a white-owned and predominantly white shop was okay:

> It was all right. There was one guy they said was prejudiced. I don't know. He didn't say very much. If we were fooling around, he wouldn't take a lot of that fooling around. . . . He would take us to this room, he'd say, "Don't bring them over here into my section. Stay in a different section."

> I: *How did you leave?*

> I got fed up with it. . . . I was expecting something like $8/hour, when I went to that cabinet-making job I was pretty disappointed — it paid a minimum wage of $3.50 at that time.

Carlton admitted that his friends liked fooling around: "I was trying to stay out of trouble; I didn't get into real big trouble. We had air hoses all over the place. We would hook up different tools and stuff to the air hoses and [once we] blew a bottle up, a plastic bottle — it burst." I imagined that, under the circumstances, this antic might have been sufficient to get the three students fired. But Carlton explained that there seemed to be an ulterior motive for keeping them employed, at least on the books. He did not go into detail, but rather explained that he and the other students became suspicious when they realized that they were not being trained in the fashion that they had been led to believe was typical for their positions:

> I: *Did you get in trouble for that one? Did you almost get fired?*

> No, we didn't get fired, they wouldn't fire us. I think there was some kind of scam or something because we were apprentices. They said they were supposed to take us to a school or something and give us training, but they didn't, and we talked with some of the workers on the job who were apprentices also, and they went to school.

> I: *White guys?*

> Yes.

Carlton continued: "They failed to really train us—as a matter of fact, they zapped us out of the skills we did have because we weren't exercising our skills, we weren't doing what we were supposed to because we were sweeping, sanding, and stuff. . . . Four of us were apprentices and the rest of them were pretty skilled. They knew what was going on."

THE INFORMAL AND FORMAL WORK-STUDY PROGRAMS

White male teachers at Glendale are not uniformly helpful to white students or uniformly hostile to black students. Instead, they seem, to differing degrees, to be encouraging and supportive of both groups. They seem genuinely dedicated to the job of transmitting skills that prepare students for vocational careers, and they commanded the respect of the majority of students with whom I spoke. Nevertheless, there is a discernable unequal pattern in the strategies that are used to assist white and black students.

The modal pattern for white teachers and students involves the active and frequent extension of teachers' personal resources to assist white students in getting within-trade jobs and work opportunities, particularly in teachers' own small businesses, that are not generally available to all students. As a result of this kind of assistance, a number of white males began acquiring very early in their career experience within trade and related fields, tools necessary for many jobs, and funds to purchase or maintain vehicles. In addition, white male students' personal network portfolios were broadened considerably when teachers linked the young men to personal contacts who could facilitate younger men's entry. These contacts included teachers' former students, family members, friends, and of course the teachers themselves.

In contrast, the modal pattern for black students and white teachers — who were in many cases the same ones who gave munificent, concrete, network-based support to white students — involved verbal support and encouragement, and frequently only that. Sometimes they offered assistance in getting formal work-study opportunities through city-run programs, such as Commonwealth Plus or the work-study office. However, white teachers did not refer black students to any of their personal contacts, nor did they employ the black students I interviewed in their own businesses. Often, teachers did no more than allow students to miss classes for half a day, while Ms. Williams or a Commonwealth Plus staff member handled interview and work arrangements.

While Ms. Williams was highly regarded by these students, neither she nor the black students she served were a part of any longstanding networks of white employers. The white students either didn't know who she was or saw her as a rubber stamp for their informal arrangements. In many ways, white families, students, and employers seemed to perceive both Ms. Williams and Glendale's black students as irrelevant intruders.

Local whites own many of the small and medium-size businesses in fields like construction, automotive services, and plumbing, which provide work-study opportunities and full-time jobs for Glendale graduates.

Because of their informal network contacts, as well as racial preference, young white students at Glendale apparently have an inside track to jobs that are routinely thought to be available only by way of standard interviews and institutionally-certified qualifications. For black Glendale students, even those who come highly recommended, neither what nor who they know make much difference in terms of early opportunities in the school-work transition.

SEVEN

Networks of Inclusion, Networks of Exclusion

The Production and Maintenance of Segregated Opportunity Structures

Some men leave their sons money, some large investments,
some business connections and some a profession. I have none
of these to bequeath to my sons. I have only one worthwhile
thing to give: my trade. . . . For this simple father's wish it
is said that I discriminate against Negroes. Don't all of us
discriminate? Which of us when it comes to choice will not
choose a son over all others?

— Benjamin Wolkinson

Young men, if they are lucky, navigate the passage from school to work buoyed and guided by supportive institutions and individuals. In Chapter 6, we saw that black Glendale men mainly relied upon formal job placement mechanisms and the encouraging words of some of their white male teachers, while white students were able to count on material assistance from these same teachers, to the point where they scarcely needed formal job placement assistance. These in-school differences accentuated conditions outside of school. In the mono-racial homes and neighborhoods of the Glendale men — stable working-class and lower-middle-class communities — white men were surrounded by and included within networks of gainfully employed older white men, who gave them additional material assistance. That is, phone calls and spaces were made for them, they were included in neighborhood carpools, sponsored by those with connections to bosses and foremen, called for side jobs, guaranteed interviews or hired on the spot, and trained and socialized by older men who saw them as sons or younger brothers — and so overlooked their early mistakes and mischievous adolescent antics. They were deemed by friends and often strangers as worthy, irrespective of their mediocre school records or brushes with the law.

Black Glendale men had contacts too — older blacks, like Ms. Williams, who tried to lend a hand. But those who provided assistance frequently could only point out openings — not make informal phone calls or hire the person outright, bring a young man to a job site, or introduce him to an employer at a barbecue and get him a job that day, if he wanted one. Frequently black men's contacts were black women, who had few, if any, connections to blue-collar trades. Only on rare occasions were older black men in a position to hire younger black men for trade work, and then only for one or two side jobs rather than full-time, year-round work. In my comparisons of how black and white men used networks, I also noticed that the contacts who assisted black men were more careful, more circumspect in their assisting efforts.

Both the content of networks, in terms of well-placed contacts, and the ways in which contacts can exercise influence differ significantly for blacks and whites. White men can approach a multitude of well-placed contacts who can provide significant assistance relatively effortlessly and with little cost attached, while blacks must rely on poorly placed contacts who must be careful to examine the costs and rewards of using their meager influence. In Chapter 6, we saw that having access to white male teachers did not guarantee, or even increase the likelihood, that black men would establish racially integrated networks. Instead, even within school, black and white networks remained distinct, and there is no reason to expect this pattern to be reversed outside of school. Outside of school, where working-class people's ties are not expected to go beyond family, neighborhood, community, or race, they generally don't. Older white men, who are the best contacts, conscientiously recruit and support younger white men in the better blue-collar jobs, and while training them, driving them to work, or chatting during a job, they socialize these younger men to racial and other "realities" as they perceive them. The idea of reverse discrimination — the preferential hiring of minorities and women over white men — is a perception that enjoys growing currency among such whites.[1] Its embrace all but guarantees that neither older nor younger white men will share their rich social capital — capacity to command resources and access through contacts — with blacks, who, in this perspective, can only be seen as competitors — competitors assisted by hated government policies.[2]

In the context of telling their job-search stories, both black and white students registered complaints about how they were faring in Baltimore's job market. Some black students complained about racial discrimination at the hands of white employers, but many also blamed themselves for their career difficulties. White men, who were extremely successful compared to their black peers, nonetheless expressed frustration at not having achieved more. Several white students thought that racial quotas had limited their occupational options, giving their black peers an advantage over them. None of the white students saw themselves as uniquely advantaged compared to their black peers, not even those who acknowledged having seen black workers put up with harassment on the job. Black men revealed experiences in which racism was made explicit — as when white workers called them "niggers" — and others in which its implicit presence, like suspicion, hung heavy in the air. As Ms. Williams noted, some black men had begun to search, consciously and unconsciously, for employment sites in which they were, if not the majority, at least a stable presence. The men, by virtue of separate social worlds, had penetrated distinct labor markets: one dominated by longstanding networks of white men, the other by a far more random assortment of people.

In this chapter, I compare the efficacy of the personal contacts of the graduates, examine how the young men perceived the significance of racial preference as a career obstacle, and draw conclusions about differences in the content, operation, and overall usefulness of black and white men's networks. Because I am particularly interested in assistance that resulted in jobs in trade fields, for the remainder of this analysis I eliminate most of the Miscellaneous students, who are attending community or four-year colleges full-time. Note, however, that many chose the community college option not as a result of being on the fast track, but rather as a result of failure of their job search. This is especially the case with black men. One of the best ways to see how networks are differentially efficacious for these men is to conduct comparisons within the remaining success categories — that is, to compare men who, on the face of it, appear to have similar achievements. It becomes apparent that, even at the lowest levels of success, white men's networks connect them with desirable training and occupational options, which remain open (on stand-by) even while they pursue other objectives or simply fool around. Black men lack similar options, and instead exhaust the usefulness of their limited networks in the first few years out of high school.

THE LEAST SUCCESSFUL TRANSITIONS: LIMITED CONTACTS AND STALLED CAREERS

Six of the Glendale graduates had a particularly hard time in their school-work transitions. Among these graduates, none had gotten a job within their field and, with only one exception, none was stably employed at the time of the interview. But even among these students, there were significant differences between the one white male student, Timothy Brice, and his five black peers.

Tim, like at least one of his black peers, Craig Mourning, seemed more interested in pursuing a music career than in pursuing work in his trade, auto mechanics. Yet Tim had held a number of jobs, which he had found as a result of assistance provided by personal contacts. For example, Tim got his first job at Pizzaweel, a pizzeria near Johns Hopkins. Tim explained, "I used to work there for my cousin's boyfriend, who owned the place." His second job, not surprisingly one of his favorites, was at the Record House at a local mall. Again, Tim's contacts helped him. When I asked how he got the job, he nonchalantly replied, "I just applied. I knew some people there and I interviewed with the manager." Tim worked at the Record House for nearly three years and then quit because of management changes. After working on the Harbor Shuttle Taxi for a summer, Tim got his current job at the Casual Cafe. Tim explained, "My friend's brother owns it and he offered me a job there and I said yes, so I've been there about a month."

Tim planned to stay at the Casual Cafe for the foreseeable future, in the hope that if his friend's brother opened another restaurant, he would be selected as the manager. Although Tim at that time earned only about two hundred dollars a week, including tips, he was reasonably certain he would receive raises once he had been on the job for a few more months. Tim knew a number of apprentices and union members in the electrical field and said that he would consider attempting an electrician's apprenticeship with the help of some of his friends if for some reason neither his musical career nor his restaurant management options materialized.

Three patterns are evident in this brief rendering of the career path of Tim, the only low-success white male. First, Tim used his contacts routinely to pursue jobs that he wanted. Second, Tim's contacts included owners and others who had the power to decide who was interviewed and who was hired. Third, Tim knew tradesmen who could get him into a highly remunerative electrician's apprenticeship program, even though his original trade was auto mechanics. These features of Tim's network made it likely that he would be able to weather a potentially unsuccessful effort at a musical career, and even be able to switch to the electrical trade without significant difficulty at some time in the future.

Two of Tim's black peers, Jared Martin and Jerome Foreman, provide a useful contrast to Tim's experiences. Neither had the kind of connections with owners or tradesmen that Tim had, nor were they able to use less powerful contacts as effectively. Both Jared and Jerome had an interest in auto mechanics, but neither had studied the field while at Glendale. At the time, Jared was enrolled full-time at Lincoln Tech, a rather expensive ($7,000 per year) automotive technology school. Jared's parents helped him with tuition. He had studied industrial electronics while in high school and had hoped to begin an entry-level industrial electronics job after graduating, but he was never recommended for work-study and had no contacts within the field. Although he was unemployed at the time of the interview, he had held three jobs in his life: grill cook at McDonalds, cashier at Seven-Eleven, and catering attendant for Marin's, a local chain of banquet halls. Jared said he got those jobs through walk-in applications, and currently was looking for jobs with the assistance of Antoinette Green, a black employment officer at Lincoln Tech. Jared did not know any apprentices or union members, but he said that a couple of his brothers and cousins currently worked as automotive technicians. They suggested that he attend Lincoln Tech. It was clear to him from the reports of his contacts that such training would be necessary before Jared could be recommended and have any hope of attaining a job in the field.

Jerome Foreman was the only black male who'd spent time in prison: he had served two years for possession with intent to sell cocaine. [Two white students had been convicted and served time in prison, one for aggravated assault and the other for possession of drugs with intent to sell, like Jerome.] He had been released a few months before the interview and had not reestablished himself. Although Jerome's record showed that before his prison stint he never held a stable job in the business trade he had studied, he explained to me that he had mainly worked informally (off the books) as a mechanic in a small neighborhood shop. Mark Davies, a white shop owner, occasionally hired him to do simple work on cars, and sometimes Jerome did work on his own in the neighborhood. Jerome did not have any other significant contacts and stated that he felt his prison record would probably make it difficult to accumulate contacts in the future. He'd had no work-study jobs and did not expect to return to the business field any time soon.

Two of the least successful black students, Craig Mourning and Jamal Hines, had studied and performed well in traditional trades (electrical construction and industrial electronics, respectively) while at Glendale. Both had held a number of jobs — none within their training fields — and both were unemployed when I interviewed them. Unlike their white peers (some of whom I discussed in the last chapter), neither of these men had significant contacts who had actually helped them to get jobs. Instead, their contacts — all workers rather than supervisors or owners, no tradesmen in their fields, and no union members or apprentices — provided minimal assistance. Craig, for example, mentioned his grandfather and one cousin who gave him minimal assistance and two female contacts, a godsister and his mother, upon whom he was equally likely to rely. In Craig's case, an interesting pattern emerged regarding his contacts, who made suggestions that seemed disconnected from their own work places. For example, Craig's grandfather helped him get a job application — but not for the company where the grandfather had worked. In addition, the job was not accessible by public transportation, so Craig never applied. Similarly, the cousin told Craig about a job; however, the cousin did not work there and had simply seen an ad in the paper.

All of Craig's jobs so far have been in the low-wage service sector, such as stock clerk, kitchen helper, and packer. His highest wage has been $5.00 per hour, but most of his jobs have been minimum wage — even the one that he got with the help of a friend. He explained how a contact at Jansen Square Food Market helped him to land a stock person's job: "It wasn't no application involved in this; I got this job because I knew one of the guys that worked there, I knew a guy that worked around the store." But most of Craig's jobs have come as a result of his diligence with newspaper ads and walk-in applications.

While Craig pursued a number of job leads — nearly always by bus —

he also worked on perfecting his rapping techniques. Because of his religious background, his rapping style tended to be positive and uplifting rather than militant and critical of society. He'd gotten a couple of "gigs" rapping and several more as a disc jockey and shared one of his tapes with me, but so far neither his rap career nor his disc jockeying had taken off. Craig had been unemployed for a few months at the time of the interview, and he seemed somewhat depressed, as he was having to rely on his grandparents, who, like him, did not have transportation, and who were living on a small fixed income.

Jamal had also been unemployed for a few months and living in Baltimore County with his wife and small child when I interviewed him. He had received disability insurance for a few months after being hit by a school bus on the way to work, but had not been able to assume his old position after recovering. He had held a number of jobs — kitchen cleaner, busboy, driver, security guard, truck loader, bowling alley attendant, and a one-day job as a pin checker at a bowling alley, which ended because of a racial incident.

Racial discrimination was not the only problem Jamal faced. He had attempted to get security guard training and certification at a private school. The school arranged a loan of $2,300, charged to Jamal but going directly to the school, to pay for his training. As I mentioned in an earlier chapter, after receiving minimal training, Jamal applied for a job at a drugstore, only to find that there was no listing for the school he had attended. Jamal, however, was still responsible for repaying his loan. Jamal had friends who might be able to help him get a job in an office, but none of his friends, he says, could help him get the kind of job he was interested in and for which he felt qualified.

Another of the least successful black students, Ricky Benton, had been employed only in a city summer jobs program connected to the Commonwealth Plus program since leaving Glendale. At the time of the interview, he was working as a receptionist for a black male teacher who administered the Commonwealth Plus program during the summer. Ricky was earning $4.25 an hour (the most he'd ever earned) and desperately hoping that the job could somehow be made permanent. While a student, Ricky studied food services and got a work-study in the twelfth grade with Special Times Catering, a black-owned firm. He was still relying on his mother for transportation and was frustrated that he couldn't get his own informal catering business off the ground, though he'd done a couple of parties and church functions. I spoke with Ricky's stepfather, a city sanitation worker, who seemed genuinely supportive of Ricky's culinary efforts; he explained that he didn't think Ricky would get a break in the catering business unless he attended a culinary institute, which the family could not afford at the time of the interview.

In the lowest success category, only Tim Brice, a white male student, mentioned business owners and tradesmen who had offered to assist him in getting training or jobs in the city. None of the low-success black males had been able to create connections with those who hire entry-level workers, nor did they know tradesmen who could assist them in gaining access to apprenticeships or union jobs. Indeed, none of the black men's contacts, including family members and more casual or "weak" ties, had been able to provide even jobs the men could subsist on until something better came along — as Tim's friend (whose brother owned the Casual Cafe) had done.

MODERATE SUCCESS IN BLACK AND WHITE

Moderate success within and outside of the original trade field was the modal category for blacks. Ten of the twenty-five black graduates I interviewed fell into this category — but only one of the ten had gotten a job within his field. Only three whites fell into the moderate success category, and two held jobs in their training fields. I'll start with the white graduates.

Sean Mullino, Alex Henley, and Chuck Hartman were the only white students, other than Tim Brice and some of the full-time students, whose earnings did not exceed $8.00 an hour. Sean's earnings were the least stable because he was employed mainly as an off-the-books construction worker. Alex and Chuck had both received wage increases within a few months of the interview and expected to get raises within the next few months, so they might have ended up in the higher success categories within a short time. Each of these young men was assisted by older white males in getting jobs, and all three seemed pleased with some aspects of their early career experiences.

Sean, an electrical construction student, had been working informally in the construction business since graduating. He explained that if he had not at the same time been attempting to begin a musical career, he would have had no problem finding work in the city of Baltimore, where his and his father's construction contacts were impressive. He explained,

> I had a friend of mine who was in construction and I would just go help with drywall jobs for him — that was like throughout different days during the summer, here and there. It wasn't really steady. It was under the table, which is what I do now. I don't have a steady job now.
>
> *I: But you're working?*
>
> Yes, on and off.

I asked Sean how he'd gotten a job working as a maintenance man at Merry-Villa, a nuns' retirement home.

> My father worked at . . . he's still working at Trace Hardware. He works in the back doing the charging accounts, and this guy Frank is the maintenance guru over at Merry Villa. So he comes in and [Dad] says, "My kid just got laid off from whatever," and Frank says, "Tell him to come on down here and talk to the nuns." So next thing I know. . . .
>
> *I: Dad helped?*
>
> Actually, the conversation between them was like, "The boy needs work," and Frank was like, "Have him stop on down." I had just got my license, I didn't have my own car yet and I was still using the old man's. I dropped him off at work, so when I dropped him off in the

morning and Frank was there waiting to get some parts, he says, "Come work for me, let's go down and talk to the nuns." My father worked at the hardware store and always had the introduction to tools, and I knew basically everything that I needed to fix.

I: So they hired you on the spot?

Yes.

Sean further explained how he'd go about getting side jobs if he needed extra money:

What I would do is use any connections through my father and say, "Hey pop, is anybody coming into the store who needs a ceiling fan put up?" Considering that an electrician, what a regular electrician would charge a person — $75 to come in and another $100 in labor, a couple hundred dollars in parts — I can undercut them quite easily and still come out with like $200/week if I can do that.

Printing student Alex Henley had been working at a printing job since graduating. Alex credited his girlfriend's parents with getting him the job, as they knew the owners of the company and arranged an interview for him. Although Alex had been with the company for only a couple of years, he was somewhat concerned that his wage was only $7.00/hour. Alex had decided to stay with the company only because he had an extensive health benefits plan and paid vacations, which he said compensated in part for what he lacked in wages.

Like Alex and Sean, Chuck Hartman was also assisted by a girlfriend's parent and his father. Describing how he'd gotten a job with Prenney's, he said, "My mother-in-law now . . . I was dating her daughter so . . . she needed a security guard and I needed a job." Even a low-paying janitorial job Chuck got came through friends and family. As he explained, "I knew some of the guys that worked down there, and my uncle was my warehouse manager — he told me to go down there and try, and the guy said, 'I'm just getting ready to lay my janitor off — if you want the job, it's yours.' So I took it. Start pay was $5.50, and I think I was making $5.75

when I left." Next Chuck moved to a bar and restaurant supply company called Flack's, and from there got his current job as a delivery truck driver. Men within his growing network assisted each transition:

> My dad worked with them [Flack's owners]. It seems like everybody I know is always getting me a job. Flack's went out of business and before they went out of business I went to another company that we used to purchase all of our stock off of and got myself a job — Silters.

I: How did you get the job at Silters?

> I knew the owners down there, I'd been down there plenty of times buying stuff for the other company, so I went down there, and they knew that I was there everyday at work for the other company so they just gave me the job and said they were hiring for drivers.

Although these white students did not seem aware of it, their accomplishments, even in the moderate success category, exceeded those of the black students. For example, all of the black students except one were working outside their training fields. Tony Price, a food services student, had managed to get a job working in the delicatessen of a black-owned grocery store, thanks to his family doctor (also black), who called the store owner to recommend Tony. Tony was pleased with both the work climate and the modest benefits package his job provided, even though his wage was only $5.70/hour.

The other nine black students had tried to find jobs in their fields but eventually settled for what they could get. To a man, they lacked the rich supply of within-field contacts white students had. Two students who had studied auto mechanics, Kenneth Richardson and Dion Banes, became salesmen: one sold sporting goods, the other, automotive parts. Jermaine Decker, a brick masonry student, and Allen Hairston, a carpentry student, found jobs as delivery truck drivers. Two other students, Gary Garfield and Larry Fisk, who had studied industrial electronics and printing, respectively, wound up working as banquet hall attendants. At the time of the interview, Gary was making a transition from banquet hall work to a more promising job as a part-time auto mechanic. He was also pursuing a third job (on Saturdays) selling sports equipment. Kahari Moore, a third auto mechanics student in the moderate success category, combined two jobs, one as a dietary porter and another as a PBX operator. Like Gary, Kahari managed to achieve moderate success (by my criteria) by holding two part-time jobs at the same time. Another black auto mechanics student, Terrence Hall, seemed poised for higher success in the future, since he had gotten a job as a residential counselor for mentally handicapped youth. His state job offered a modest salary but a fairly extensive benefits package.

Most of the black men got their jobs through walk-in applications and newspaper advertisements — far more rarely through word-of-mouth. Even when contacts helped, the assistance was minimal, such as pointing out a job in the paper or offering a ride to an interview. Unlike white peers, few were significantly assisted by members of their network. None of the black men had been significantly assisted by whites in their job searches, and many had to rely on female contacts who had better access to service sector, as opposed to blue-collar, fields. Carlton Fields's example provides a case in point.

Carlton studied carpentry at Glendale but, aside from an unsuccessful work-study experience, had worked only infrequently on occasional side jobs with his uncle Billy. Carlton explained, "He does jobs on the side and sometimes when he needs help or something . . . I will call and ask him if he needs help on the side. He does a lot of stuff, he rearranges rooms, he did a job building decks . . . home improvements." Carlton's mother helped Carlton and a few of his brothers and sisters get jobs as hall attendants for Mascot Catering, where she had worked for several years. Carlton didn't have a car, so he rode to work with his mother. Carlton described his work environment as integrated, but explained that his supervisors were all white, while most of the other attendants were black. Carlton felt that since graduating, he had begun to lose some of his carpentry skills. He still hoped for a job in the maintenance section of his workplace, where he could fix things and hone some of his construction skills, but so far he had only learned about food preparation and display.

SWITCHING GEARS AND LANDING ON YOUR FEET:
HIGH SUCCESS OUTSIDE OF FIELD

The modal category for white male students was achieving high success outside of their field; ten of the twenty-five students fit in this category. Only three of the black students fit the pattern, but I begin with them because they provide important insights into the unique obstacles even relatively successful blacks face.

Two of the black students, Walter Brown (auto body) and Junior Rivers (electrical construction), managed to get jobs setting up displays. Walter's job at a convention center involved setting up dance floors, display tables, and stages, while Junior delivered and set up Pepsi displays in local grocery and convenience stores. While both enjoyed their display jobs, neither had made satisfactory headway into their trades. At the same time, both Walter and Junior had better within-field connections and experiences than most black students who had trained in auto mechanics and electrical construction.

Junior, for example, had been hired by his uncle Bullet, who owned a very small construction company. Junior's uncle, an electrical shop teacher in Baltimore County, had started a part-time business, not unlike those Junior's white male teachers owned. But Junior did not like working for his uncle because work was never plentiful enough to provide a stable wage. In addition to his uncle, Junior listed Jerry Woods as someone who he could call for employment assistance. He had not yet called "Uncle Jerry," a friend of his late father's who worked as a quality control technician at Sparrow's Point, but instead had relied on his friend Roy Jones. Junior's experiences with "Cousin Roy" highlighted a constraint on black contacts that I never observed operating for whites: although Cousin Roy had alerted Junior to a job opening in his firm and provided significant information about the duties and expectations for the job, he indicated that mentioning their connection to the hiring supervisor could be a liability. Ordinarily mentioning one's contact is the way to "cash in" — the key for getting in the door. In every instance, this is how it worked for the white men I studied. But Junior, who did succeed in getting a job in the distribution section, was told not to mention his friend during the interview. Other black men revealed similar cautionary tales, but Junior's was especially vivid. As he explained,

> He [Roy Jones] said, "Well, they're hiring this week." They only hire on certain weeks, and he basically told me what the job was going to be. When I went in there, I was over the top of everybody. I knew more than anybody else in there because of him. [Before] I didn't have any idea what a merchandiser job was.

> I: *Did he help you in getting an interview or getting the job itself?*

> He told me who to talk to. . . . He said just tell him I was interested in the job.

> I: *And that he sent you?*

> No, I didn't say that. The key thing when you go down to Pepsi — they [black workers] say, "Don't say you know nobody; they [white managers] don't like hiring people like that."

Apparently, Pepsi recruits workers mainly through internal labor market processes, since Junior was sure that he would not have even heard about the job were it not for Cousin Roy: "Down there, they put a job opening on the board, and you won't see it in the paper, like, he had to tell me when they were hiring. Basically, you have to know somebody to tell you when they're hiring." Junior also explained that the interview was only the beginning of a tedious application process. He had to take reading and math comprehension tests and a physical, including a drug test. According to Junior, "It wasn't like they just said, 'You're hired'; we went through a whole lot."

Junior learned a great deal from the application process and from his contact's careful instructions. Most importantly, Junior learned to use his potential as a contact carefully and sparingly. I asked Junior if he had helped others to get a job with Pepsi. He explained that he was very hesitant to help others because he felt his reputation might be at risk if he recommended someone who didn't work out: "I don't want to try and get anybody in and then they get in and mess up, you know what I mean, like [his bosses might say], 'What happened? I thought you said he was a good guy.'"

Walter, the other display technician, had held two jobs in the auto body field, one before he graduated and one right after. Walter said he left the field because few shop owners were willing to provide retirement benefits and health insurance, and since he was married and his wife was expecting a baby, both were major concerns for him. He was the only black student who received work-study assistance from a white shop teacher (he'd been recommended and had gotten jobs twice), but Walter had found his current job through his father's contacts. As he explained, "My father, he works for the city, he's a supervisor, he put in a good word for me. His supervisor went to our church, and he knew what type of person I was . . . he has a little pull. He helped me get the interview, but the rest was 'up to me,' he said." Walter did not plan to return to the auto body field. Instead, his plan was to establish a long career with the city, where he hoped someday to become a supervisor like his father.

The third black student who fit the High Success Outside Field category was Darnell Curtain, president of the 1989 senior class. At the time of the interview, Darnell, a business student who had gone on to study accounting at Murphy State University, was working as a residential counselor at the Hackey School, a school for troubled adolescents. I asked Darnell how he got the job, and he explained: "I'm part of a choir group [at Murphy State University], and one of the founding fathers [Brian Key] of the group is a team coordinator out there. . . . I knew Brian and the manager who hired me, Henry Jones, he was the unit manager of the unit I'm presently working on." Darnell participated in another social group with Brian, Henry, and a number of other employed black men. Darnell had no white contacts but felt that the older black men of his social group would serve as an effective and supportive network throughout his career.

Several of the nine white students who achieved high success, but not in the fields for which they trained, worked directly with or for their parents or other close relatives; even where this was not the case, most of their jobs came through friends or neighborhood connections. Norm Louganis, for example, worked for a firm partly owned by his father; the other owners are Greek coethnics. He reports that "I get along real good with [his supervisor]. I don't want to say employer to employee, I say good friends." Norm said he could expect a good future with the company and that he would "most likely get bumped up," since his father was part owner. Naturally, Norm did not have to go through any sort of interview process. Asked if he would need a resume for other jobs, he explained, "I wouldn't have no resume to show exactly what I could do, but my father, he knows exactly what I can do." Norm summed up the company's hiring practices as: "It was like nepotism, all Greeks!"

Jeff, a brick masonry student who had just completed a stint with the army, is the atypical white student, since he achieved high success without extensive family assistance. His jobs had come through acquaintances and teachers. He got his first job — as a bricklayer — because he knew the president of the company. Subsequent jobs came through teachers whom he thought of as friends. Even a minor job he held as a sample person for a supermarket came as a result of someone's help. He explained, "I knew the girl's mother who was the supervisor." At his current job, where he works as a stock clerk for a large warehouse-style department store, his father knew the personnel manager — but Jeff assured me that no calls were made on his behalf. Calls from his father were probably unnecessary, though, since Jeff already knew Herb, his boss's boss, before he got the job. Jeff saw his supervisors and others positioned higher within the company hierarchy as friends, since he regularly accompanied them on camping and hunting trips. But Jeff did not see these personal relationships as contributing to his success. Instead, Jeff suggested that he had been warmly accepted because many of the managers were "in the army and we had that in common."

One highly successful auto body student, Chip Kazinsky, made significant contacts while he worked with his friend Kurt Bolton (another white respondent) at a restaurant that served as a "watering hole" for many white union members. Like Kurt, Chip turned down high school work-study jobs that were arranged by his shop teacher, but had a job working with the Tri-State construction company before graduating. Chip knew he'd fit into the company, since he'd worked on side jobs during the summer months with the owner, Neil Ryder, beginning around the tenth grade. As Chip explained it, "I just about knew the whole company. They'd all get off of work and they'd come into the bar, and they'd always sit there and I knew them." In addition to unionized construction workers, Chip also befriended members of the printers', steamfitters', and electricians' unions. He said that, given his connections, it wouldn't have been a problem for him to pursue apprenticeship in any one of these trades.

Danny O'Brien, a white brick masonry student, had used both family contacts and friends to establish himself. In his litany of jobs, he listed contact after contact. Danny's first job was working for his father's business, a service station and parking garage. His second job was with Carvel's Ice Cream; he was hired by his sister's mother-in-law. His third job came from his teacher, Mr. Spano; his fourth job, as a busboy, came through a friend of the family's; his fifth job, at Johns Hopkins, came because "My Dad knows everybody at Hopkins." Sixth, he did side jobs, again for his ex-teacher, Mr. Spano. His seventh job, putting up fences for Steadfast Construction, came both through an ad in the paper and because he had a friend who worked there. At the time of the interview, he installed burglar alarms, had been there for six months, and was hired by the vice-president, whom he knew. He "was talking to the V.P. one day and he told me they needed a helper and I went and worked as a helper . . . hired me on the spot."

Like Danny, who admitted to having sold drugs in high school, two other white students, Dean Costner and Oscar Stokes, had been in trouble with the police while in high school, yet still managed to get extensive help from members of their networks. Oscar, a printing student, had managed to land on his feet, after being arrested a number of times and serving some jail time, by relying on friends, neighbors, and family members. His first job, with an insulation company, came as a result of his brother's and uncle's help: "My brother and uncle worked there and they just needed a helper and they just got me the job and I started going to work with them." Oscar had run-ins with the boss's brother at the insulation job, which he left and then returned to after serving a short sentence for assault with a deadly weapon and malicious destruction. I asked Oscar how he managed to stay employed given his bad record. He explained: "Brothers, uncles, friends — I know about fifteen people from this neighborhood — a lot of them are cousins, people's kids. The guy that owns the place [where he currently works] grew up in Critchfield [Oscar's neighborhood] . . . and he hired his buddies." Oscar also knew union members in the printing trade who had offered to get him into a printer's apprenticeship, but he was no longer interested in pursuing the trade.

White auto mechanic student Dean Crawford had served prison time for grand theft auto, but currently worked as a highway construction laborer. I asked Dean how he went from auto mechanics to construction. He said, "I'm good friends with the foreman there, I grew up with his brother." Two of Dean's neighbors, Scott and Tim, had also helped Dean to get his current job, which paid high union-scale wages. Even though he had his own car, Dean usually rode to work with Scott. Consequently, if he were to lose his source of transportation, Dean most likely wouldn't have to give up his job, even though the job sometimes required travelling two hours to get to the job site.

Three other white students (Jay Oldman, Doug Daniels, and Micky Allen) fit the same basic pattern, with variations. Most of their jobs, especially their better jobs, came through friends, family, or neighbors. Their contacts, all employed white males, had already proven effective in connecting them to desirable employment opportunities outside their trade fields. Some of the men even had significant within-field contacts who could assist them in reentering their trades, if they so desired.

THE HIGHEST LEVEL OF SUCCESS:
APPRENTICES MAKING IT IN THE TRADES TRADITION

Students who pursued and got apprenticeships either with unions or nonunion firms had the most successful early experiences within their trades. These students took a path that resembles the school-work pattern in countries like Germany, except that their transitions were coordinated far more often by significant individuals (mainly personal contacts) than by institutions. In the United States, policy makers regularly attempt to create incentives for schools, unions, and firms to make these sorts of transitions more the rule than the exception.[3] The ways in which young men in my sample made these transitions have implications for how such incentives might (or might not) work. A total of seven white students and one black student fit some variant of the apprentice pattern. Again, personal connections are a key to acquiring these coveted jobs.

White student Ron Curtis, for example, had a highly coveted job as an apprentice at Baltimore Gas and Electric (BG&E), a job that some white students insisted would never go to a white.

> Dave Kotchenreuther. He's a friend of my father's, and they grew up together since they were knee-high, and he worked at the gas company. He's always been around here, we go crabbing and fishing together and stuff. He always looked up to the way I carried myself and had my future planned out, and he told me, like four hours out of school there might be a chance of getting a work-study here, but that didn't go through because they weren't hiring. But the next time the job openings came around, he let me know. I got my resume together, he turned it in for me and I had to wait awhile.

He had to wait two or three months but then was called in for an interview, hired, and started at $11.68 an hour. Had he not gotten this job, Ron reports, he could have asked his uncles for help: all five of them are electricians, and one has his own business. His father, also an electrician, is a union member.

Other highly successful white students who stayed in their original trades — Josh, Dan, and Max — also used rich family-centered networks, which were highly efficacious. Josh Schacter was discussed in an earlier chapter as a student who had received considerable help from his shop teachers. He now works in the family business. His oldest brother, Jack, is the vice president of Schacter Enterprises and has his master electrician's license; Josh is supervised by his brothers Jack and Mark, and reports that the family is "very close-knit." Dan Waring, a service technician earning $10.00/hour, has had only one job since graduating. Teachers helped him get it, but he could also have worked with his father, a refrigeration engineer, as his brother did. Max Wilson has a job as an auto mechanic, arranged by his brother.

Connections and family are important, even when family members do not hold the coveted position. Kurt Bolton, for example, was able to enter the electricians' union as an apprentice with the assistance of his father's friend, Jack Morseburger, a local restaurant owner. Jack was an electrician before he opened the restaurant, his brother Richard continues to be an electrician, and the restaurant is a hangout for electricians and officials of the local union. Kurt explained to me that the restaurant is an important social space for older white male unionists, and that being there helped him to get connected:

> As far as what Jack and Richard did, like everything, it's politics,
> there's people to see. It's not what you know; it's who you know.
> So some people can pull more weight than others, some more in
> the local than others. They've got friends. Owning a restaurant,
> the [union] committee comes up there all the time, and that's great.
> When I was applying for the apprenticeship committee as I was
> working, they came in twice when I was working there. Jack made it
> so I was working that night and I served the crabs, I did the shrimp,
> my face got known and I got known. So you get recognized . . .

Only one black man, electrical construction student Hank Searles, breaks the usual pattern for black men by having significant older white male contacts. Hank was mentioned by his white and black peers as being particularly good in the field of electrical construction, but that Hank had nonetheless experienced chronic difficulties with his shop teachers. Despite those interactions, on work-study jobs that Hank got on his own (while still in high school), he earned the respect of a few white tradesmen, with whom he has kept in touch. He described an especially close relationship with Dave, an older white tradesman whose home he had never visited, but with whom he nevertheless felt close. He spoke of Dave almost as a friend, as did many of his white peers when referring to their senior contacts. Describing his role as Dave's helper, he said: "[It] was more than just assist, we shared everything, we went together everywhere just about. He told me what to do and I did it, but we shared everything." Hank credits Dave with providing most of his trade training, but Hank left the job working with Dave for another that paid better. The new job required that Hank work for two older white men who had been "high up" at the previous job, where he worked beside Dave. He considers both men solid references if he were interested in returning to electrical or construction work.

Hank was told by some of the white men he worked with that he was "different." While he suggested that he understood this comment to mean different from typical blacks, Hank, a Jehovah's Witness, credited his difference to his religion: "I would give all that credit to my religion making me different." But Hank *is* different — from all of his peers — in the way he approaches employers and conducts himself while at work. For example, unlike any of the white or black men I met, Hank *always* goes to interviews (for electrical construction jobs) in a suit and tie. He also saw his attitude as key: "I'm always smiling. I'm always in a good mood — I go to work and some guys cuss [playfully] at me because they say I'm always in a good mood, and they say, 'Why can't I be like that?'"

However, Hank's carefully constructed self-presentation did not keep him from experiencing problems. In the field, Hank explained, people made racially offensive remarks "all the time." According to Hank, "They thought it was okay with me because I was so cool with them, so they used to say stuff." Hank was accustomed to tolerating a great deal of these kinds of remarks, much of it couched as humor, but at some point, he said, "That was enough." This choice and ability to tolerate to a point was underscored in many of Hank's comments. According to him, it's important "to know how to take jokes, but also if they offend you, you've got to let them know some kind of way, but you've got to know how to take it when it's really not offensive, it could be just a small joke." If a black person did not know how to do this, Hank said, "It would be tough." Managing banter and cross-race interactions, he said, "is very crucial because most of the time when you go on an interview, it's a white person interviewing you, not a black person, and you've got to be ready for it."

Despite Hank's demonstrated skill at these interactions, he said that if he could avoid it he would not return to electrical construction (union or nonunion) if it involved working with white men. Instead, he had taken a job as a cable installer. Hank was able to get this job (and several earlier ones) with little or no assistance from personal contacts. He explained the appeal of the current job: "At this job too — by me being a subcontractor, I have no boss and I love it. . . . [The bosses] basically don't tell us what to do because we're out in the field, we don't see them all day . . . so it's basically independent, that's what I like about it." By the time of the interview, Hank had acquired a van and hired one of his black classmates to assist him in installing cable in Baltimore County. Hank's experiences are instructive: despite his considerable success getting jobs in the electrical field, he found the pressures and (racial) animosity so wearing that he opted to leave the apprenticeship and take a job that probably holds less long-run promise but enables him to work on his own. Hank's experiences with racial discrimination, many of which were mirrored and amplified in the comments of his black peers, make understandable his choice to forego construction work for the independence of cable installation. But I couldn't help wondering if his white trade contacts would eventually forget him, making traditional trade reentry a less viable option over time.

RACIAL PREFERENCES, REAL AND IMAGINED

Both black and white men claimed that racial preferences had hindered their employment efforts. Black men's claims were usually linked to firsthand experiences in majority white firms, while white men's claims tended to emerge as a result of hearsay about quotas favoring blacks. I almost didn't ask white men if they felt they had experienced discrimination at the hands of employers, because I thought they might react badly. I was glad that I chose to ask after the white men began to express fears of having lost significant opportunities as a result of perceived favoritism toward blacks. Nearly all of the white men in the study mentioned "reverse discrimination" in one form or another during the interviews. The contrast was striking between the personal experiences of the black men and the vivid fears of the white men. Several black men expressed frustration with the treatment they received from white males in the job interview setting, on the job, and sometimes even in training settings. In one instance, electrical construction student Craig Mourning described applying for a food service job with J. Bryers and Sons, which he wasn't able to get as a walk-in. Craig suspected that his initial rejection resulted from racial discrimination, since he was later able to get an interview after reconnecting with the Commonwealth Plus Program.

> J. Bryers — the Commonwealth got me the job. You know what's funny about that, I knew one guy that worked there, Ricardo Boyd. He told me they was hiring. I went down there, dressed up for an interview, filled out an application and — "Sorry, we're not hiring anymore." I went home and for a couple days [heard nothing] and [then] I get a call back from Commonwealth Plus — "J. Bryers and Sons are hiring." I just went down there. Well they hire now. I went down there and I got the job from them, but me coming in one-on-one, no.
>
> *I: Why?*
>
> Why do I think I didn't get the job? I'm black.

Although his current supervisor is a white woman with whom he gets along well, carpentry student Carlton Fields's boss (the person who is authorized to hire and fire hall attendants) is a white male who Carlton suspects of being prejudiced: "My boss, the manager Jack Scoffield, he's prejudiced. He can't be bothered to speak to black people. He put a lot of people down." Carlton did not elaborate on his boss's behaviors, but he was not the only black student who mentioned difficulties getting along with white supervisors.

Brick masonry student Jamal Hines described a number of racial incidents, one at a bowling alley,

> There was one I had for one day, that was for a bowling company, Stanley's, I think. I worked for them while I was in school but when I moved out here [the suburbs] I went to the one out here to get a job. I worked there one day, I ran into some serious problems.

> *I: Tell me.*

> They served alcohol in there and I don't know, this is a predominantly white area and the guys would be drinking and certain words were said and when I approached the person about it the manager yelled at me.

> *I: What did they say?*

> He said words that I don't like to repeat, he said a couple of things. ["Nigger" was one of the words.]

Jamal reported several other experiences with racial discrimination and felt that one of the greatest barriers to his success "is my color, but I wouldn't change that." Most of the discrimination is not open and absolute, but covert and deniable. A white boss refused to have a direct conversation with Jamal, the company's only black employee. A white worker whom he thought of as his friend told Jamal that he just needed to maintain a pleasant demeanor, explaining, "You are the ones that are always smiling. . . . You can go a long way if you do what I just told you." In another case, he was blamed for a coworker's mistake:

I worked at JL's, and the night supervisor, Beau Duster [and the owner], . . . they were unloading and everything was on the ground and they were putting them on the skidder. So I was driving the skidder into the warehouse, and he [Duster] put a box on upside down and it shifted the whole load. It didn't fall. I took it in real slow and I set it down and I started working on it. So the owner of the company, you know, "What are you doing with this? Why did you break this up?" And I told him [Duster had stacked the boxes] and he went back to Beau [Duster] and he said, "Why did you try to stack the boxes? You stacked it wrong." He said, "Oh, that was that nigger."

In contrast, most white students focused on opportunities they imagined to be foreclosed to whites like themselves. In fact, it is clear that their impressions were wrong; the students involved, however, insisted that their views were based on firm evidence, and in some cases the operation of the system worked to create and sustain that impression. Four men, Chip Kazinsky, Jay Oldman, Dan Waring, and Sandy Butz, spoke in detail about this issue. While most of their comments concerned preferences for blacks, women, and other minorities, Kurt, a white electrician's apprentice, also reflected on the difficulties that black apprentices faced in his local. Three of the white students were convinced that they could not get police officer jobs within Baltimore County because of quotas designed to include women and minorities.

Although Chip was pleased with his current job, he complained that he had suffered racial discrimination when he tried to get a state police job. His comments provide a sample of the pervasive fear of antiwhite discrimination that I observed among the white students, and also demonstrates the way whites in positions of authority use racism to make their job easier. Rather than telling white applicants they have been rejected on their merits, rather than explaining that a great many white applicants had better credentials, unsuccessful white applicants are told that the reason for their rejection is a preference for black applicants.

I applied for State Police and I passed all the tests and stuff like that. And we were down there for something, I forget what it was. And one of the state troopers (we were on the side, a group of white male individuals), he said to us — we obviously weren't selected to go further in preemployment — he said, "I'm sorry, fellas. Unfortunately, if you were black you would have had the job."

I: How did that make you feel?

It didn't make me feel any less of a person because I knew that I had the potential to get the job. I just feel that our system is a little bit screwed up the way sometimes . . . where it feels that it's obligated to certain minorities to give them a certain amount of jobs for each job. I feel — I'm working on the old system — you could get the job according to the qualifications. So I wouldn't expect to go down to a drafting company and have a guy who's got CAD [computer aided design] training not get the job over me because I was black. As far as that goes, I feel there's a lot of discrimination against that. I feel you should be hired for your intelligence, not for your race.

I: How did the other guys react?

They were — "Fucking niggers!" — and all this bullshit and it was like there is nothing you can do about it. These guys were like, "What can we do about it?" They said, "You've got to vote and stuff like that." And they were like, "Vote? We don't want to vote, we just want to be hired."

For the whites involved in these sorts of interchanges, this is a win/win situation. The white applicant wins: he (or sometimes she) is reinforced in his (or her) belief that on merits he or she would succeed. The only reason he or she is not being hired is the racial privilege (supposedly) possessed by black people. Other forms of privilege disappear: no attention is directed to the hiring of white relatives, the use of political connections, or friendship networks within the police force. Nor is any attention given to the many white applicants who, on strictly meritocratic criteria, had stronger records, so that even if a number of whites had been hired, it would not necessarily mean that this applicant would get a job.

The white trooper (or other employing agency official dispensing bad news) wins because he has found a way to deliver the news such that he and his agency will not encounter any hostility, despite the fact that they are rejecting applicants. Things would not have gone so smoothly if the trooper pulled applicants over to the side to say to them, "I'm sorry, fellas. We only had twenty-five places; two of them went to the sons of troopers, three went to cousins and neighbors, one went to a political connection, four were reserved for minority or female applicants (and, frankly, those applicants had really strong records), and we had tons of great applicants for the remaining fifteen positions. In fact, we had three hundred applicants with scores higher than any of you." Instead, in the trooper's formulation — a formulation used by a great many employers who reject white applicants — both the applicant and the employer/rejector are victims of a larger social force, affirmative action. The white applicant who is told that were he black he would be hired directs his hostility at a powerless racial group, black people, rather than at the employing agency, the person delivering the bad news, the test used, or the qualifications demanded. The rejected white applicant is also spared the need to blame himself or to feel that he has not measured up by universalistic standards. The consequence is that white students believe, based on what they were told, that they were denied a job solely because of race.

Dan Waring, a successful industrial electronics student, was hoping to transfer into law enforcement but worried that being white would hurt his chances. When I asked him what the greatest barriers to his success were, he exclaimed:

Quota systems!

I: Where they have to hire more minority candidates?

Exactly . . . Like, for instance, the state has to hire like 90 percent minorities and 5 percent women, and you're left with like 5 percent or 3 percent white males.

I: Why do they have to do that?

It's a federal law. Then when you have three thousand people applying and they're only accepting sixteen people, then your [i.e., white
men's] chances are really cut. A couple of years ago when Baltimore
County was hiring, [they got] three to four thousand applications
and they only accepted sixteen people, so with all the quota systems
you're left with like a 3 percent radius. That's really tough. I don't
have a problem with who they hire, I just think they should hire the
best qualified person for the job regardless.

Note how peculiar this analysis is. The white student identified "quota
systems" as the greatest barrier to his success, but by his own account
there were 3000–4000 applicants for 16 positions. If there were 3200
applicants, and *no* blacks were hired, Dan Waring would have had a 1 in
200 chance of being hired, that is, 0.5%. Even if we accept his (incredi-
bly unlikely and totally unsupported) claim that 90 percent of these 16
positions went to black applicants, then 0.4375 percent of applicants
were rejected because of the "quota" and 99.5 percent were rejected
because there were so many applications for so few positions (with
0.0625 percent hired strictly because of their merit). By far the most
important barrier was too many people chasing too few positions.

Jay Oldman, a former auto mechanics student who has a job as a city
police officer, registered concerns similar to Dan's when I asked if he'd
ever experienced racial discrimination:

Yes. Because at first I wasn't going to go to the city. I was going to
the county, but they have to hire so many minorities first. They hire
blacks to meet their quota and then they'll hire whoever else [after].

I: Were you afraid that if you applied you might not get the job?

I know some people who did work for Baltimore County and they
did get in. The city — you don't have that problem, they are more
or less leveled out. You know there is around fifty-fifty in the city,
whereas the counties still have to meet their quota because they are
short of the minority — it's not just blacks, it's minorities in general,
females, blacks, Asians, and then they get to you [white males].

I: At that point, would you expect to wait longer to hear back from them?

I expected they probably wouldn't even hire me, they'd find funny things not to hire you.

I: Did you actually apply for the county?

I decided not to.

It is difficult at this juncture to evaluate some elements of these stories. Jay Oldman "knows people," presumably whites, who did get the county jobs he and Dan Waring said were not available to men like themselves. Because state police forces historically discriminated against black applicants, it is possible that the state police are currently under pressure to rectify this past abuse; even here, the evidence consists solely of unattributed hearsay and a statement by a white officer trying to break the news to unsuccessful white applicants. To return to the example of the police officer providing bad news, if ten out of twelve officers hired had been whites with connections on the force (like Jay Oldman), what would we expect the police officer to say? He might easily have focused on the two black officers hired. His remark contained no concrete or specific evidence of numbers hired, test scores, or the like — nor did he ask the group of white applicants about their qualifications prior to making his comment. The comment nonetheless was accepted by Chip and the others as a definitive assessment.

In another instance, my data seemed to contradict the impression of one of the white students. Sandy Butz, one of the highest paid electrician apprentices, was convinced that apprentice slots with Baltimore Gas and Electric were reserved for black males. Yet Ron Curtis, one of Sandy's white classmates, had held a BG&E apprenticeship after graduating from Glendale. Another white student, Kurt Bolton, said that he had been offered an apprentice position with BG&E also, but turned it down to become an apprentice in a local much like Sandy's.

Since Kurt was accepted into an electrician's union local, he knew who had been included rather than relying on vague and misleading impressions. In addition, his anxieties were probably reduced by the security of a good job, the one he wanted. As a result of both factors, he had a more realistic sense of how racial preference worked in his local. He explained:

> Took a year before I could get accepted.

> *I: Why?*

> Because they only let a certain amount of people in a year. I think the year I got in they only allowed forty people in. Of course, you've got to take care of the relatives, families and minorities first and then they pick from people — the top 5 percent of the people that apply.

> *I: How many slots are left after they take care of relatives, families, and minorities?*

> It depends on how many they have. This year in my class, maybe they have fifteen slots left.

> *I: How many would you estimate go to minorities?*

> I have a class of about twenty-five, and there are three women, four black men, the rest are white males.

Although Kurt didn't claim that he'd been the victim of discrimination, he expressed greater concern about the acceptance of black male apprentices than either better connected white males or females. He seemed especially concerned about blacks who he felt used the presence of racism in American society to justify claims for special treatment:

> There are people who know that they're the minority, and they're the people who know that "you need me, I'm the token black, I can do whatever I want. And there ain't nothing you can do about it." . . . It's a shame that the racism is out there, and it's a shame that people know it's out there and they use it. . . . Instead of helping their people, all they're doing is creating a bigger stereotype.

Here Kurt suggests that although racism against blacks is a problem, some blacks manage to gain power and flout the rules.

At other points in the interview, Kurt expressed concern for black workers who face racial harassment, particularly black apprentices within his local:

> When I was working at the mall, there were a couple of black apprentices, and they weren't getting their fair shakes because the foreman was white and he would come over to us and make jokes. A lot of guys agreed, but I'm not really a prejudiced person.
>
> I: *What did you think?*
>
> I think — I don't like it.
>
> I: *When you're a journeyman, will you be willing to work with a black apprentice?*
>
> Yes, I worked with a black journeyman.
>
> I: *Do you know a lot of them?*
>
> No, because there aren't a lot. But the black apprentices in my class are good. The black guys in my class don't have any problem. . . . I'd be afraid of a lot of things if I was a black guy. . . . I'd be nervous just because of the way it is, but if I was black I'd know how to deal with it. The guys in my class know how to deal with it.
>
> I: *You said that if you were a black guy you'd be scared of other things — what would you be scared of?*
>
> Other things — a lot of things nowadays. The work environment, everybody always looking down on them, I see it.

Kurt seemed willing to grant the black apprentices he knew a sort of "honorary white" status, perhaps because he respected how they coped with various, potentially tense, racial situations.

> The guys in my class, I don't look at them like they're black, I look at them like they're just regular guys. Of course, we have the black guy jokes and all that kind of stuff. We have this thing in one of our books, it's a safety thing that has this guy tripping over ladders, falling over steps, just doing stuff that [isn't] safe. The way the copy

is run off, the guy looks black and one of the guys [apprentices in his class] who is black goes, "You notice this is a black guy here making all these mistakes and falling, don't you?" You just laugh because he's just kidding.

RACED NETWORKS: "INVISIBLE HAND(S)" MADE VISIBLE

Other things being equal — and in this study they are — the stronger one's network, the better one's chances of making stable labor market transitions. No group has been more powerful in Baltimore's blue-collar trades than older white men. As a result of older white men's assistance, the white men in this study had better and smoother passages from school to work than their black peers. In every case — from lowest to highest achievement — white men's labor market penetration and resilience was enhanced through ties with older same-race men. Only one black male was connected to older white tradesmen, and those connections had already resulted in access to several electrical construction jobs, the highest wage rate and lowest unemployment rate among the black men in the study, and offers of assistance to pursue apprentice programs. But Hank Searles's choice to become an independent cable installer, rather than pursuing the construction trade, may already have put at risk his ability to maintain and use the cross-racial ties he established while in high school. In addition, because he did not live near or socialize in the white neighborhoods of his white mentors, few opportunities existed for casually reestablishing connection. All of the other black men relied on less well placed black women and men, none of whom were in a good position to assist with blue-collar job entry.

"Networks," according to Powell and Smith-Doerr (1994), "do the valuable work of matching supply and demand; they transmit through personal communication information that is not circulating through public channels."[4] Networks determine "how individuals are linked to one another and how these bonds of affiliation serve as both lubricant for getting things done and a glue that provides order and meaning to life."[5]

Because older white men actively recruit and assist younger white men — even those who are not family members, to the virtual exclusion of young black men — patterns that unfairly advantaged white men during the pre–Civil Rights era continue to do so now. And the pattern is multilayered.

At every network layer, white men are at an advantage compared to black men. There is a difference in both the ways in which networks function and the types of contacts to which the men can gain access. While black men mainly rely on workers, white men know both workers and bosses (or those who do the hiring). White contacts are able to make recommendations without having to consider racial patterns in the job setting, while black contacts must do so. White contacts can recommend young men for jobs in which the men have little or no training. Black contacts can recommend young men only when the men have evidence of training or expertise in the field. White men with contacts can be hired for desirable blue-collar jobs without interviews. Black men with contacts will be interviewed for all but the most menial jobs — and sometimes those too. With each job held, white men increase the density of their networks — the numbers of and overlaps between contacts. Black men occasionally expand their networks by a few people, usually other blacks who can provide minimal assistance. White men rely upon more experienced and more successful older white tradesmen. Black men rely upon less successful black tradesmen or friends and relatives who are not connected to the trades. White contacts pay a smaller price than black contacts for recommending young workers who don't turn out well. Young black workers may be instructed to downplay their contacts rather than mentioning them explicitly — as most white men can and are encouraged to do. Young white workers are neither permanently ejected from nor unduly stigmatized within networks if they "act out" or get into trouble. Young black men must be extra careful not to confirm widely held stereotypes regarding their alleged irresponsibility and unfitness as workers. Young white men get many of their first experiences working in the small businesses of family members or neighbors, where mistakes can be quickly and quietly corrected. Young black men's first jobs may be in white-owned firms where early mistakes confirm racially biased suspicions. Less well connected white men acquire useful contacts in effectively segregated settings — taverns, parks, neighborhoods, and restaurants — in which blacks are not welcome. In all of these ways, older white men's blue-collar dominance is passed on to younger white men, essentially replicating a once purposeful, now perhaps unintentional, structure of exclusion that kept prior generations of black males out of the most lucrative blue-collar jobs.

Today, visible hands reproduce racial inequality — *invisibly*. Raced networks do not appear exclusive to white beneficiaries, who believe that, these days, too many desirable opportunities go to minorities. White men described the job process as meritocratic if they got the job, but as unfairly biased in favor of blacks if they didn't or suspected they wouldn't get the job. Generally unaware of their black peers' difficulties on the labor market, white men seemed to believe that race was more of a help than a hindrance. The combination of unintentionally exclusive practices (undisturbed customs) and an ideology of reverse racism most likely served as a strong disincentive against making any proactive attempts to include black men within predominantly white networks. As a result, the school-work transition for white men ultimately contributed to a preexisting structure of exclusion for black men, whose poor employment showing is an indication of the segregated network structure's efficacy and rigidity.

EIGHT

White Privilege
and Black Accommodation

Where Past and Contemporary
Discrimination Converge

One narrative, the achievement ideology, asserts that formal training, demonstrated ability, and appropriate personal traits will assure employment access and career mobility. The second narrative, the contacts ideology, emphasizes personal ties and affiliations as a mechanism for employment referrals, access, and mobility. As Tilly argues, the achievement ideology has persistently dominated American understanding of occupational success, even though everyone, it seems, is willing to admit that "who you know" is at least as important as "what you know" in gaining access to opportunities in American society. All of the men in this study, for example, said that contacts were very important in establishing young men like themselves in careers. One offered a more nuanced explanation: "It's not [just] who you know, it's how they know you." That is, it is not simply knowing the right people that matters; it is sharing the right sort of bonds with the right people that influences what those people would be willing to do to assist you.

The black and white men in this study had more achievements in common than contacts. They were trained in the same school, in many of the same trades, and by the same instructors. They had formal access to the same job listing services and work-study programs. Instructors and students alike agreed, and records confirm, that in terms of vocational skills and performance, the blacks and whites in this sample were among the stronger students. Yet the Market approach (the achievement ideology) fails to account for the divergent employment outcomes among the Glendale graduates.

Black Glendale graduates trail behind their white peers. They are employed less often in the skilled trades, especially within the fields for which they have been trained; they earn less per hour; they hold lower status positions; they receive fewer promotions; and they experience more and longer periods of unemployment. No set of educational, skill, performance, or personal characteristics unique to either the black or white students differentiates them in ways that would explain the unequal outcomes described in Chapters 4 and 5. Only their racial status and the way it situates them in racially exclusive networks during the school-work transition process adequately explain their divergent paths from seemingly equal beginnings.

In this study of one variant of the "who you know" versus "what you know" conundrum, it is manifestly and perpetually evident that racial dynamics are a key arbiter of employment outcome. Yet challenging the power of the achievement ideology in American society requires a careful exposition of how factors such as race throw a wrench into the presumption of meritocracy. In addition, the contacts ideology must be uniquely construed to take into account the significance of racially determined patterns of affiliation within a class, in this case the working class.

RACE, AN ARBITER OF EMPLOYMENT NETWORKS

Researchers have long argued that black males lack access to the types of personal contacts that white males appear to have in abundance.[1] I would argue that it's more than not having the right contacts. In terms of social networks, black men are at a disadvantage in terms of configuration, content, and operation, a disadvantage that is exacerbated in sectors with long traditions of racial exclusion, such as the blue-collar trades. Even when blacks and whites have access to some of the same connections, as in this study, care must be taken to examine exactly what transpires. For example, I noted that black and white males were assisted differently by the same white male teachers. If I had only asked students whether they considered their shop teachers contacts on which they could rely, equal numbers of black and white males would have answered affirmatively. But this would have told us nothing about *how* white male teachers *chose to know and help* their black male students. The teachers chose to verbally encourage black students, while providing more active assistance to white students. I discovered a munificent flow of various forms of assistance, including vacancy information, referrals, direct job recruitment, formal and informal training, vouching behaviors, and leniency in supervision. For white students, this practice, which repeated neighborhood and community patterns within school walls, served to convert institutional ties (as teachers) into personal ones (as friends) that are intended to and do endure well beyond high school.

I had thought (and hoped) that schools like Glendale might serve as a cross-pollination point for the personal networks of young black and white men. However, I detected no explicit efforts to create cross-racial connections among the men, and I am sure, given their comments to me, that some white students and their families would have openly challenged, subverted, or avoided such efforts. Even without teachers consciously discriminating, significant employment information and assistance remained racially privatized within this public school context. In that white male teachers provided a parallel or shadow transition system for white students that was not equally available to black students, segregated networks still governed the school-work transition at Glendale even though classrooms had long been desegregated.

The implications for black men are devastating. Despite having unprecedented access to the same preparatory institution as their white peers, black males could not effectively use the institutional connection to establish successful trade entry. Moreover, segregation in multiple social arenas, beyond schools, all but precluded the possibility of network overlaps among working-class black and white men. As a result, black men sought employment using a truncated, resource-impoverished network consisting of strong ties to other blacks (family, friends, and school officials) who like themselves lacked efficacious ties to employment.

Beyond school, matters were even worse. Without being aware of it, white males' descriptions of their experiences revealed a pattern of intergenerational intraracial assistance networks among young and older white men that assured even the worst young troublemaker a solid place within the blue-collar fold. The white men I studied were not in any way rugged individualists; rather they survived and thrived in rich, racially exclusive networks.

For the white men, neighborhood taverns, restaurants, and bars served as informal job placement centers where busboys were recruited to union apprentice programs, pizza delivery boys learned to be refrigeration specialists, and dishwashers studying drafting could work alongside master electricians then switch back to drafting if they wished. I learned of opportunities that kept coming, even when young men weren't particularly deserving. One young man had been able to hold onto his job after verbally abusing his boss. Another got a job installing burglar alarms after meeting the vice president of the company at a cookout — without ever having to reveal his prison record, which included a conviction for burglary.

Again and again, the white men I spoke with described opportunities that had landed in their laps, not as the result of outstanding achievements or personal characteristics, but rather as the result of the assistance of older white neighbors, brothers, family friends, teachers, uncles, fathers, and sometimes mothers, aunts, and girlfriends (and their families), all of whom overlooked the men's flaws. It never seemed to matter that the men were not A students, that they occasionally got into legal trouble, that they lied about work experiences from time to time, or that they engaged in horseplay on the job. All of this was expected, brushed off as typical "boys will be boys" behavior, and it was sometimes the source of laughter at the dining room table. In other words, there were no significant costs for white men associated with being young and inexperienced, somewhat immature, and undisciplined.

The sympathetic pleasure I felt at hearing stories of easy survival among working-class white men in an era of deindustrialization was only offset by the depressing stories I heard from the twenty-five black men. Their early employment experiences were dismal in comparison, providing a stark and disturbing contrast. Whereas white men can be thought of as the second-chance kids, black men's opportunities were so fragile that most could not have recovered from even the relatively insignificant mishaps that white men reported in passing.

Black men were rarely able to stay in the trades they studied, and they were far less likely than white men to start in one trade and later switch to a different one, landing on their feet. Once out of the skilled trade sphere, they sank to the low-skill service sector, usually retail or food services. The black men had numerous experiences of discrimination at the hands of older white male supervisors, who did not offer to help them and frequently denigrated them, using familiar racial epithets. The young black men I spoke with also had to be careful when using older black social contacts. More than one man indicated to me that, when being interviewed by a white person, the wisest course of action is to behave as if you don't know anyone who works at the plant, even if a current worker told you about the opening. These young black men, who had been on the labor market between two and three years, were becoming discouraged. While they had not yet left the labor force altogether, many (with the help of parents) had invested time and resources in training programs or college courses that they and their families hoped would open up new opportunities in or beyond the blue-collar skilled labor market. Many of the men had begun to lose the skills they had learned in high school; others, particularly those who'd had a spell or two of unemployment, showed signs of depression.

My systematic examination of the experiences of these fifty matched young men leads me to conclude that the blue-collar labor market does not function as a market in the classic sense. No pool of workers presents itself, offering sets of skills and work values that determine who gets matched with the most and least desirable opportunities. Rather, older men who recruit, hire, and fire young workers choose those with whom they are comfortable or familiar. Visible hands trump the "invisible hand" — and norms of racial exclusivity passed down from generation to generation in American cities continue to inhibit black men's entry into the better skilled jobs in the blue-collar sector.

Claims of meritocratic sorting in the blue-collar sector are simply false; equally false are claims that young black men are inadequately educated, inherently hostile, or too uninterested in hard work or skill mastery to be desirable workers. These sorts of claims seek to locate working-class black men's employment difficulties in the men's alleged deficits — bad attitudes, shiftlessness, poor skills — rather than in the structures and procedures of worker selection that are typically under the direct control of older white men whose preferences, by custom, do not reflect meritocratic criteria.

Few, if any, political pressures, laws, or policies provide sufficient incentives or sanctions to prevent such employers from arbitrarily excluding black workers or hiring them only for menial jobs for which they are vastly overqualified. Moreover, in recent years, affirmative action policies that required that government contracts occasionally be awarded to black-owned firms or white-owned firms that consistently hire black workers have come under attack — eroding the paltry incentives for inclusion set forth during the Civil Rights era, nearly forty years ago. Indeed, there is far less pressure today than in the past for white-owned firms to hire black working men. And given persistent patterns of segregation — equivalent to an American apartheid, according to leading sociologists — there remain few incentives for white men to adopt young black men into informal, neighborhood-generated networks. As a result, occupational apartheid reigns in the sector that has always held the greatest potential for upward mobility, or just basic security, for modestly educated Americans.

IDEOLOGY AND THE DEFENSE
OF RACIALIZED EMPLOYMENT NETWORKS

The public perception of the causes of black men's labor difficulties — namely, that the men themselves are to be blamed — contrasts with my findings. And my research is consistent with that of hundreds of social scientists who have demonstrated state-supported and informal patterns of racial exclusion in housing, education, labor markets, and even investment opportunities. Racism continues to limit the life chances of modestly educated black men.

Yet many whites seem more concerned today about what they perceive as "racism" directed against them rather than forms of racism that they perpetuate or from which they simply benefit. The fear of becoming victims of racism, among the traditionally dominant racial group, sets the stage for a reinvigorated defensive posture. Understandably, the legitimate fear of losing easy jobs in an era of downsizing makes the maintenance of and perhaps increased reliance upon old-style exclusionary practices seem a rational response to dire conditions. But another rational response is cross-racial organizing among all vulnerable workers. The effort to create a multiracial class-based solidarity has been undermined by the sense of proprietary interest many whites demonstrate regarding jobs. When whites speak of "them" taking "our" jobs — jobs for which no one has yet competed — they assume jobs *rightfully* belong to another white person, irrespective of whether blacks and other people of color have competitive qualifications.

Whites like those I interviewed believe that although blacks may not know the right local people, they have the advantage of "knowing" public officials who promote powerful and intrusive government mandates for their inclusion. In this view, racial preferences form the bases of contact advantages, which are thought to exclude white males in favor of blacks, irrespective of meritocratic criteria. Many of the white men I studied were convinced that "quotas" (i.e., desegregation and equal opportunity or affirmative action programs) for the inclusion of blacks were severely limiting white employment prospects. Many felt they, as whites, were the victims of racial preference or exclusion. The perception of whites as underdogs vis-à-vis black economic competitors was pervasive among the working-class white men I studied. However, I was struck by their faulty logic: since black males do not dominate the trades and their associated unions, or even have a significant presence there, the notion of white underdogs is perplexing. Nor are older white males, who *do* control the trades, known for their receptivity toward young blacks. They have never been known to encourage integration in formal or informal ways, so there must be a different basis for whites' perceptions.

I think the underdog perception may be related to the increasing participation of blacks, women, and other minorities in public sector jobs traditionally associated with working-class white men, such as police officers, firefighters, and to a lesser extent postal workers and school officials. Student comments led me to believe that this reasoning is very persuasive. But generalizing patterns of black inclusion within the public sector to the private sector is not an accurate assessment of either legislative victories or cold, hard reality. Similarly, a growing black presence in formerly all-white trade schools and as job candidates (but rarely employees) in traditionally white industrial firms does not constitute significant encroachment on working-class white males' employment opportunities. Though no one in my study came right out and said it, I detected a logic that went along the lines, "First they (blacks) went for public sector jobs, now they are coming for private sector jobs — we're doomed if we don't hold the line against them!"

White men in the trades, though they may be somewhat aware of the patterns of racial exclusion or accommodation to which black men are subject, need not acknowledge to themselves or to others that the obverse of black subordination is white privilege. Inflated perceptions of black success, bolstered by reverse discrimination arguments, provide an ideological basis for not recognizing — for actively denying — contemporary privileges that are racially determined. To the extent that such ideologies currently dominate working-class white men's culture, crude arguments about black inferiority are not needed to maintain exclusion. Instead, ideological conviction of black ascendancy and of powerful forces that unjustly advantage blacks make it morally permissible — perhaps even morally mandatory — to differentially assist whites. These ideologies, coupled with the exclusionary behaviors they legitimate, provide a contemporary deathblow to working-class black men's chances of establishing a foothold in the traditional trades.

WHITE PRIVILEGE, BLACK ACCOMMODATION

How, then, do black males, if they wish to earn a living in the surviving trades, negotiate training and employment opportunities in which networks of gatekeepers remain committed to maintaining white privilege? The present research suggests that the options are few: either accommodation to the parameters of a racialized system or failure in establishing a successful trade career. The interviews revealed that forms of black accommodation begin early, as when young men avoided training in trades of interest because they were known to hold little promise for integration and advancement. For those who made such discoveries later, accommodation took the form of disengaging from specific trades, such as electrical construction, and pursuing whatever jobs became available. For some, the disengaging process involved the claim that they were never really committed to the original trade field, but I suspect that such claims merely served to soften the blow of almost inevitable career failure. For the determined, accommodation required suppressing anger at racially motivated insults and biased employment decisions in the majority-white trade settings. If this strategy wore thin, two difficult accommodations remained. The first involved finding a work setting — not necessarily within one's trade — in which the workplace culture was, if not actively receptive to black inclusion, at least neutral. The second involved finding ways to work in white-dominated fields without having to work beside whites.

A word needs to be said about a particularly troubling accommodative behavior adopted by the black men: not actively and persistently pursuing offers of assistance. It is not clear to what extent the black men were fully cognizant of the extent and potency of whites' informal networks or of the cultural norms governing their operation. But, while it is evident that the older white men who were network gatekeepers did not extend the same access and support to the black men, the black men may also have been less proactive in pursuing older white men who might have assisted them.

Generally, the white men in the study appear to have more actively followed up on offers of assistance. And although their careers developed much more smoothly than those of the black men, they were certainly not without the difficulties of not being hired, workplace dissatisfaction, competing vocational interests, and unemployment. Nevertheless, they returned, sometimes repeatedly, to contacts for further assistance. Certainly, demonstrating proactivity toward a typically racially exclusive white network would be especially problematic for black men.

Undoubtedly, black men's exclusion from white personal settings where easy informal contact is facilitated, like neighborhoods and family, contributes to black men's reluctance to pursue whites for assistance. In addition, black men's lack of personal familiarity with normative expectations among whites probably hampers their efforts to imitate their white peers' more forward network behaviors. Furthermore, any efforts by blacks to engage in such behaviors might not be similarly regarded as appropriate, and might instead be interpreted as aggressive, "uppity," or indicative of a feeling of entitlement. Finally, black men's early experiences of racial exclusion, bias, and hostility in the school and the workplace inform not only their assessment of employment prospects, but also their actual employment strategies. Given these complicated contingencies, perhaps the somewhat hesitant responses of black men are, on the whole, not unreasonable.

CONCLUSION

Black men have paid a great price for exclusion from blue-collar trades and the networks that supply those trades, but they have not paid it alone. The pain of black men's unemployment and underemployment spreads across black communities in a ripple effect. Less able to contribute financially to the care of children and parents, or to combine resources with black women or assist other men with work entry and "learning the ropes" on the job, black men withdraw from the support structures that they need and that they are needed to support emotionally as well as economically. The enduring power of segregated networks in the blue-collar trades is as responsible as segregated neighborhoods for the existence of extremely poor and isolated black communities and of the disproportionately black and male prison population — in fact, more so. While many black families live in stable communities that are mostly, if not entirely, black, the inability to find remunerative jobs that do not require expensive college training makes living decently anywhere extremely difficult. And the loss of manufacturing jobs cannot account for black men's underemployment in the remaining blue-collar fields — especially construction, auto mechanics, plumbing, computer repair, and carpentry.

One question remains: Could affirmative action policies be used to fully desegregate the trades at this late date in the long history of exclusion? My short answer is: of course. Affirmative action policies have significantly increased the presence of modestly educated minority men vis-à-vis their white peers in at least three important arenas in the last four decades: the military, the public sector, and as apprentices, workers, and subcontractors on many government jobs. In each of these arenas, gains are directly related to the implementation of inclusive affirmative action policies.

The U.S. military began the process of desegregating in 1948, when President Truman, under pressure from black activists like A. Phillip Randolph of the Brotherhood of Sleeping Car Porters, signed Executive

Order 9981, which ended official segregation. This did little to help black soldiers win their fair share of opportunities during those first two decades, but with time, the mechanisms of recruitment and career progression became formalized and thus fairer to all soldiers, especially minority ones. Of the branches of the military, none has accomplished more in terms of opening up its opportunity structures than the army. At the beginning of the Vietnam War in 1962, 12.2 percent of the army's enlisted personnel were black, yet only 3.2 percent of commissioned officers were black. By 1998, blacks made up 26.6 percent of enlisted soldiers and 12.7 percent of commissioned officers. Perhaps most stunning of all have been changes at the highest levels; 9 percent of the army's generals, the equivalent of civilian CEOs, are black.[2]

More controversial than affirmative action in the military have been the policies that opened up jobs in the far more visible civilian public sector. Affirmative action policies in the civilian public sector have significantly reduced cronyism and nepotism at local, city, state, and federal levels. The policies created through affirmative action have been so useful, fair, and downright smart that many private sector employers voluntarily adopted the government's strategies as early as the late 1950s. The public sector led the way by creating and implementing policies that widened the pool of talent from which it could select. In general, affirmative action policies involved advertising job openings widely, interviewing a more race- and gender-diverse set of minimally qualified candidates, creating specific minimum qualifications for positions (not to mention criteria for advancement and termination), and using civil servant and other skill-based exams when warranted. These policies made it difficult to exclude minorities in favor of whites and began to expose the contradictions and unfairness of informal recruiting, hiring, and advancement practices. The results have been nothing short of astonishing for black workers. For example, between 1970 and 1990 the number of black police officers rose from 24,000 to 64,000. By 1982, 1.6 million blacks — one fourth of all black workers — were employed in government.

In terms of the kind of work most interesting to me and to the young men I studied — skilled trades — the greatest advances came about as the result of an affirmative action effort called the Philadelphia Plan, initiated by President Nixon in 1969. This plan — controversial from its inception — involved setting target ranges for inclusion of minorities on government construction jobs. Because of the stronghold of white tradesmen in virtually all of the most lucrative skilled trades, policy makers knew that making real changes would necessitate mandating inclusion and monitoring the compliance of firms. Because these policies were limited to government-sponsored jobs, they essentially required that public revenues be used only by firms that did not discriminate against minority workers (who, it should be noted, are taxpayers too). One of the first affirmative action policies embracing the use of goals and timetables, it required contractors working on government construction sites to ensure that 22–25 percent of plumbers, pipefitters, and steamfitters and 19–23 percent of sheet metal, electrical, and elevator construction workers were minorities. Despite tremendous opposition from white-run unions, many loopholes and few penalties for firms that didn't come close to goals, and the government running its own apprentice training programs to circumvent the power of union locals that continued to exclude blacks, the plan was adopted outside of Philadelphia, and by the early 1970s claimed successes in several large cities. According to Quadagno, in 1967 minorities made up less than 6 percent of all apprentices, but by 1973 they held 14 percent of apprentice positions and by 1979, 17.4 percent of such positions. Although Quadagno doesn't distinguish between union-run and government-run apprenticeship programs, even union-run programs accepted more minorities during this time. Unfortunately, the training efforts of the government were subsumed under public training programs that were neither oriented toward skilled trades nor able to withstand the mammoth cuts in social programs during the 1980s. In addition, ordinances that required contractors to hire minority trainees and workers and to use minority-owned firms as subcontractors on at least some government jobs have not been supported in recent Supreme Court decisions.[3]

My findings demonstrate that, without governmental initiatives that provide strong incentives for inclusion, white tradesmen will have no reason to open their networks to men of color. As a result, the work trajectories of white and black men who start out on an equal footing will continue to diverge into skilled and unskilled work paths because of business-as-usual patterns of exclusion. Although there are few precedents for intervening in the private sector, there are strong precedents for intervening in the public sector, where the tax dollars of majority and minority citizens must not be redistributed in ways that condone customs of exclusion. While activists like A. Phillip Randolph seem in short supply, today's more diverse and rejuvenated labor movement and concerned citizens should pressure the government and the private sector to actively recruit young black workers, who need and deserve access to skilled trade opportunities. Nothing would help able-bodied, work-ready, and trainable black men, like those I studied, more than a strong recommitment at the federal level to a Philadelphia Plan across major U.S. cities. And this time, I suspect that embattled white unionists might even put up less resistance. Without the government taking a lead, the young black men I studied — who played by the rules — are unlikely to ever reach their potential as skilled workers or to take their places as blue-collar entrepreneurs, as so many of their white peers are poised to do. This tragedy could have been averted. My hope is that it will be averted in the next generation.

SUBJECTS' OCCUPATIONS
AT THE TIME OF THE STUDY

LOW SUCCESS CATEGORY

Name	Race	Occupation
Timothy Brice	White	Unemployed
Ricky Benton	Black	Receptionist
Jerome Foreman	Black	Unemployed
Jamal Hines	Black	Unemployed
Craig Mourning	Black	Unemployed

MODERATE SUCCESS CATEGORY

Name	Race	Occupation
Chuck Hartmann	White	Truck driver
Alex Henley	White	Printing
Sean Mullino	White	Construction
Dion Banes	Black	Automotive parts salesman
Jermaine Decker	Black	Truck driver
Larry Fisk	Black	Banquet hall attendant
Gary Garfield	Black	Auto mechanic/Sales
Allen Hairston	Black	Truck driver
Terrence Hall	Black	School counselor
Allen Howard	Black	Truck driver
Kahari Moore	Black	PBX operator
Tony Price	Black	Supermarket deli server
Kenneth Richardson	Black	Sporting goods salesman

HIGH SUCCESS CATEGORY

Name	*Race*	*Occupation*
Micky Allen	White	Construction
Kurt Bolton	White	Electrician
Sandy Butz	White	Electrician
Dean Crawford	White	Highway construction
Ron Curtis	White	Electrician
Doug Daniels	White	Construction
Chip Kazinsky	White	Construction
Norm Louganis	White	Construction
Danny O'Brien	White	Bricklayer/Alarm installation
Jay Oldman	White	Police officer
Jeff Packer	White	Stock clerk in department store
Josh Schacter	White	Construction
Oscar Stokes	White	Insulation
Dan Waring	White	Electrician
Max Wilson	White	Auto technician
Darren Zeskind	White	Machinist
Walter Brown	Black	Display technician
Darnell Curtain	Black	Special needs school counselor
Junior Rivers	Black	Display technician
Hank Searles	Black	Electrical construction

NOTES

CHAPTER 1: INTRODUCTION

1. Lawrence Bobo and Vincent L. Hutchings, "Perceptions of Racial Group Competition: Extending Blumer's Theory of Group Position to a Multiracial Social Context," *American Sociological Review* 61, no. 6 (Dec. 1996): 951–72.

2. Derrick Bell, *Faces at the Bottom of the Well* (New York: Basic Books, 1992).

3. Mark Granovetter, *Getting a Job: A Study of Contacts and Careers* (Cambridge, Mass.: Harvard University Press, 1974); Mark Granovetter, "The Strength of Weak Ties: A Network Theory Revisited," in P. Marsden and N. Lin, *Social Structure and Network Analysis* (Beverly Hills, Ca.: Sage Publications, 1982); Margaret Greico, *Keeping It in the Family: Social Networks and Employment Chance* (London: Tavistock Publications, 1987).

4. Stephen A.Tuch and Jack K. Martin, eds., *Racial Attitudes in the 1990's: Continuity and Change* (Westport, Conn.: Praeger, 1997).

5. James E. Rosenbaum, Takehiko Kariya, Rick Setterstein, and Tony Maier, "Market and Network Theories of the Transition from High School to Work: Their Application to Industrialized Societies," *Annual Review of Sociology* 16: 263–99.

6. Ken Auletta, *The Underclass* (New York: Vintage Books, 1982); Harry J. Holzer, "Informal Job Search and Black Youth Unemployment," National Bureau of Economic Research Working Paper 1860 (1986); Jewell Gibbs, *Young,*

Black and Male in America: An Endangered Species (New York: Auburn House, 1988); William J. Wilson, *The Truly Disadvantaged: The Inner City, the Underclass and Public Policy* (Chicago: University of Chicago Press, 1987).

7. Harold Howe, *The Forgotten Half: Non-College Youth in America* (Washington D.C.: William T. Grant Foundation Commission on Work, Family, and Citizenship, 1988).

8. Richard Freeman and Harry J. Holzer, *The Black Youth Unemployment Crisis* (Chicago: University of Chicago Press, 1986); Douglas Glasgow, *The Black Underclass: Poverty, Unemployment and Entrapment of Ghetto Youth* (New York: Vintage Books, 1980).

9. Avner Ahituv, Marta Tienda, and V. Joseph Hotz, "Pathways from School to Work Among Black, Hispanic, and White Young Men in the 1980's" (unpublished manuscript); Robert D'Amico, and Nan L. Maxwell, "The Continuing Significance of Race in Minority Male Joblessness," *Social Forces* 73, no. 3 (March 1995): 969–91; Philip Moss and Chris Tilly, "Why Opportunity Isn't Knocking: Racial Inequality and the Demand for Labor," in *Urban Inequality: Evidence from Four Cities*, ed. Alicia O'Connor, Chris Tilly, and Lawrence Bobo (New York: Russell Sage, 1991); Peter Tiemeyer, "Racial Differences in the Transition to Stable Employment for Young Males," paper presented at American Sociological Association meeting, Washington, D.C., August 1990.

10. John Bound and Richard B. Freeman. "What Went Wrong? The Erosion of Relative Earnings and Employment Among Young Black Men in the 1980s," *Quarterly Journal of Economics* 107, no. 1 (Feb. 1992): 201–32; Harry J. Holzer, "Black Employment Problems: New Evidence, Old Questions," *Journal of Policy Analysis and Management* 13, no. 4 (1994): 699–722; Phillip Moss and Chris Tilly, "Skills and Race in Hiring: Quantitative Findings from Face to Face Interviews," *Eastern Economic Journal* 21, no. 3 (1995): 357–74.

11. Lawrence Mead, *The New Politics of Poverty* (New York: Basic Books, 1992); Stephen M. Petterson, "Are Young Black Men Really Less Willing to Work?" *American Sociological Review* 62 (Aug. 1997): 605–13.

12. Charles Murray, *Losing Ground: American Social Policy 1950–1980* (New York: Basic Books, 1984).

13. William J. Wilson, *When Work Disappears: The World of the New Urban Poor* (New York: Knopf, 1996).

14. Timothy Bates, "Rising Skills Levels and Declining Labor Force Status Among African American Males." *Journal of Negro Education* 64, no. 3 (summer 1995): 373–83; Jomills Braddock and James McPartland, "Applicant Race and Job Placement Decisions: A National Survey Experiment" *International Journal*

of Sociology and Social Policy 6 (1986): 3–24; Silvia A. Cancio, David. T. Evans, and David Maume, "Reconsidering the Declining Significance of Race: Racial Differences in Early Career Wages," *American Sociological Review* 61, no. 4 (Aug. 1996): 541–56; Roger Waldinger and Thomas Bailey, "The Continuing Significance of Race: Racial Conflict and Racial Discrimination in Construction," *Politics and Society* 19, no. 3 (1991): 291–323.

15. Margery A. Turner, Michael Fix, and Raymond J. Struyk, *Opportunities Denied, Opportunities Diminished: Racial Discrimination in Hiring.* Washington , D.C.: Urban Institute Press, 1991.

16. Derek Neale and William Johnson, "The Role of Premarket Factors in Black-White Wage Differences," *Journal of Political Economy* 104, no. 5 (1996): 870–71.

17. Douglas Massey and Nancy Denton, *American Apartheid: Segregation and the Making of the Underclass* (Cambridge, Mass.: Harvard University Press, 1993).

18. Jeannie Oakes, *Keeping Track: How Schools Structure Inequality* (New Haven, Conn.: Yale University Press, 1985).

CHAPTER 2: "INVISIBLE" AND VISIBLE HANDS

1. Richard Freeman and David A. Wise, eds., *The Youth Labor Market Problem: Its Nature, Causes, and Consequences* (Chicago: University of Chicago Press, 1982); Gordon Bloom and Herbert R. Northrop, *Economics of Labor Relations* (Homewood, Ill: Richard D. Irwin, 1977)

2. Rosenbaum, Kariya, Setterstein, and Maier, "Market and Network Theories "; Mark Granovetter, "Economic Action and Social Structure: The Problem of Embeddedness," *American Journal of Sociology* 91: 481–510; Granovetter, "The Strength of Weak Ties"; Granovetter, *Getting a Job.*

3. Charles Tilly, *Durable Inequality* (Berkeley: University of California Press, 1998).

4. Haywood Horton, Beverlyn Lundy, Cedric Herring, and Melvin E. Thomas, "Lost in the Storm: The Sociology of the Black Working Class, 1850 to 1990," *American Sociological Review* 65, no. 1 (2000): 128–137.

5. Robert Mare, "Changes in Educational Attainment and School Enrollment," in *State of the Union*, ed. Reynolds Farley (New York: Russell Sage Foundation, 1995); Nancy Folbre, *The Field Guide to the U.S. Economy* (New York: New Press, 1999).

6. Ibid.

7. Mead, *The New Politics of Poverty,* 148.

8. Dinesh D'Souza, *The End of Racism: Principles for a Multiracial Society* (New York: Free Press), 319.

9. Stephen Steinberg, *The Ethnic Myth: Race, Ethnicity, and Class in America* (Boston: Beacon Press, 1989); David Roediger, *The Wages of Whiteness: Race and the Making of the American Working Class* (London: Verso, 1991); Matthew Frye Jacobson, *Whiteness of a Different Color: European Immigrants and the Alchemy of Race* (Cambridge, Mass.: Harvard University Press, 1998).

10. Philip A. Klinkner and Rogers M. Smith, *The Unsteady March: The Rise and Decline of Racial Inequality in America* (Chicago: University of Chicago Press, 1999).

11. Roediger, *The Wages of Whiteness.*

12. Christopher Jencks, *Inequality: A Reassessment of the Effect of Family and Schooling in America* (New York: Harper and Row, 1972).

13. Neale and Johnson, "The Role of Premarket Factors," 870–71.

14. George Farkas and Kevin Vicknair, "Comment: The Need to Control for Cognitive Skill," *American Sociological Review* 61 (1996): 557–64.

15. Cancio, Evans, and Maume, "Reconsidering the Declining Significance of Race."

16. Neal and Johnson, "The Role of Premarket Factors," 872.

17. Tilly, *Durable Inequality*

18. Granovetter, *Getting a Job.*

19. Alejandro Portes, *The Economic Sociology of Immigration: Essays on Networks, Ethnicity and Entrepreneurship* (New York: Russell Sage Press, 1994); Roger Waldinger, *Still the Promised City: African American and New Immigrants in New York* (Cambridge, Mass.: Harvard University Press, 1996).

20. Alejandro Portes and Patricia Landolt, "Unsolved Mysteries: The Downside of Social Capital," *American Prospect* 7, no. 26 (1996): 28–31; Roger Waldinger, "The 'Other Side' of Embeddedness: A Case Study of the Interplay of Economy and Ethnicity," *Ethnic and Racial Studies* 18, no. 3 (1995).

21. James Rosenbaum, "Policy Uses of Research on the High School-to-Work Transition," *Sociology of Education* 69 (1996): 102–122; Mary Brinton and Takehiko Kariya, "Institutional Embeddedness in Japanese Labor Markets," in *The New Institutionalism in Sociology*, ed. Mary Brinton and Victor Nee (New York: Russell Sage Foundation, 1998); Victor Nee, "Embeddedness and Beyond: Institutions, Exchange and Social Structure," in *The New Institutionalism in Sociology*, ed. Mary Brinton and Victor Nee (New York: Russell Sage Foundation, 1998).

22. Tilly, *Durable Inequality*, 10.

23. Roger Waldinger and Thomas Bailey, "The Continuing Significance of Race: Racial Conflict and Racial Discrimination in Construction," *Politics and Society* 19, no. 3 (1991): 291–323.

24. Edna Bonacich, "A Theory of Ethnic Antagonism: The Split Labor Market," *American Sociological Review* 37 (1972).

25. Edna Bonacich, "Advanced Capitalism and Black/White Relations in the United States: A Split Labor Market Analysis," *American Sociological Review* 41 (1975): 34–51.

26. Bonacich, "A Theory of Ethnic Antagonism," 555.

27. Ibid.

28. Vernon Briggs and Thomas Marshall, *The Negro in Apprenticeship* (New York: JAI Press, 1965).

29. Mercer Sullivan, *Getting Paid: Youth, Crime and Work in the Inner City* (Ithaca, N.Y.: Cornell University Press, 1989).

30. Waldinger and Bailey, "Continuing Significance of Race," 293.

31. Gibbs, *Young, Black and Male in America*.

32. Donald Tomaskovic-Devey, *Gender and Racial Inequality at Work* (Ithaca, N.Y.: ILR Press, 1993).

33. Philippe Bourgois, *In Search of Respect: Selling Crack in El Barrio* (Cambridge: Cambridge University Press, 1995).

34. Michael H. Tonry, *Malign Neglect: Race, Crime and Punishment in America* (New York: Oxford University Press, 1995).

35. Angela Davis, "Race and Criminalization: Black Americans and the Punishment Industry," in *The House that Race Built*, ed. Wahneema Lubiano (New York: Pantheon Books, 1997).

CHAPTER 3: FROM SCHOOL TO WORK . . .
IN BLACK AND WHITE

1. Freeman and Wise, eds., *The Youth Labor Market Problem;* Freeman and Holzer, *The Black Youth Employment Crisis;* Moss and Tilly, "Skills and Race in Hiring."

2. Elijah Anderson, *A Place on the Corner* (Chicago: University of Chicago Press, 1978); Jay MacLeod, *Ain't No Makin' It: Leveled Aspirations in a Low Income Neighborhood* (Boulder, Colo.: Westview Press, 1987); Sullivan, *Getting Paid;* Bourgois, *In Search of Respect.*

3. Herbert S. Parnes and A. Cohen, "Occupational Information and Labor

Market Status: The Case of Young Men," *Journal of Human Resources* 10, no. 1 (1975): 44–55; Harvey Kantor and David Tyack, eds., *Work, Youth and Schooling: Historical Perspectives on the Vocationalism in American Education* (Stanford, Ca.: Stanford University Press, 1985).

4. W. Norton Grubb and Lorraine M. McDonnell, *Local Systems of Vocational Education and Job Training: Diversity, Interdependence, and Effectiveness* (Berkeley, Ca.: National Center for Research in Vocational Education, 1991).

5. *From School to Work* (Princeton, N.J.: Policy Information Center, Educational Testing Service, 1990).

6. Rosenbaum, Kariya, Setterstein, and Maier, "Market and Network Theories."

7. Oakes, *Keeping Track.*

8. Rosenbaum, "Policy Uses of Research on the High School-to-Work Transition."

9. JoMills Braddock and James M. McPartland, "How Minorities Continue to be Excluded from Equal Employment Opportunities: Research on Labor Market and Institutional Barriers," *Journal of Social Issues* 43, no. 1 (1987): 5–39.

10. Coleman, *Youth Transition to Adulthood.*

11. Hamilton, "Apprenticeship as a Transition to Adulthood."

12. Rosenbaum and Kariya, "From High School to Work."

13. Rosenbaum, Kariya, Setterstein, and Maier, "Market and Network Theories"; Hamilton, "Apprenticeship as a Transition to Adulthood in West Germany." See also Steven Hamilton, "Work and Maturity: Occupational Socialization of Non-College Youth in the United States and West Germany," *Research in the Sociology of Education and Socialization* 7 (1987): 283–312.

14. Rosenbaum, Kariya, Setterstein, and Maier, "Market and Network Theories"; Freeman and Holzer, *The Black Youth Employment Crisis; From School to Work* (Princeton, N.J.: Policy Information Center, Educational Testing Service, 1990).

15. Examples of good jobs include electricians, plumbers, construction workers, semiskilled and skilled technicians, and manufacturing jobs in industrial plants. Examples of bad or dead-end jobs include busboys, janitors, hospital orderlies, food preparers and servers, and grounds-keepers. I also hoped to find a setting that had a number of active unions and apprenticing programs.

16. Edmund Meyer, Yvonne Hadja and Bernard Levenson, *Unpublished Report for the Maryland Equal Opportunity Commission Supervised by James Coleman, Johns Hopkins University Center for the Social Organization of Schools*, Baltimore: Maryland Equal Opportunity Commission.

17. Ibid., 6.
18. Ibid., 8.

CHAPTER 4: GETTING A JOB, NOT GETTING A JOB

1. Walter Allen and Reynolds Farley, *The Color Line and the Quality of Life in America* (New York: Russell Sage Foundation, 1987); Stanley Lieberson, *A Piece of the Pie: Blacks and White Immigrants Since 1880* (Berkeley: University of California Press, 1980).

2. David Gordon, Richard Edwards, and Michael Reich, *Segmented Work, Divided Workers* (Cambridge: Cambridge University Press, 1982).

3. Melvin Oliver and Thomas Shapiro, *Black Wealth, White Wealth: A New Perspective on Racial Inequality* (New York: Routledge, 1997).

4. U.S. Bureau of the Census, *County Business Patterns, Maryland* (1960–96).

5. U.S. Bureau of the Census, *County Business Patterns, Maryland* (1983–96).

6. U.S. Bureau of the Census, *Statistical Abstracts of the United States: National Data Book* (Washington, D.C.: U.S. Government Printing Office, 1997).

7. U.S. Bureau of the Census, *County Business Patterns, Maryland* (1971–96).

8. U.S. Department of Labor, *Report on the American Workforce* (Washington, D.C.: U.S. Government Printing Office, 1997).

9. U.S. Department of Labor. *Occupational Handbook, 1998–1999 Edition* (Washington, D.C.: U.S. Government Printing Office, 1999).

10. Sullivan, *Getting Paid*.

11. Richard Belous, *The Contingent Economy: The Growth of the Temporary, Part-Time, and Subcontracted Workforce* (Washington, D.C.: National Planning Association, 1989).

12. Michael Kimmel, *Changing Men: New Directions in Research on Men and Masculinity* (Newbury Park, Ca.: Sage, 1987); Lillian Rubin, *Families on the Faultline: America's Working Class Speaks About the Family, the Economy, Race and Ethnicity* (New York: Harper Collins Publishers, 1987).

13. Holzer, "Black Employment Problems"; D'Amico and Maxwell, "The Continuing Significance of Race"; Franklin D. Wilson, Marta Tienda, and Lawrence Wu, "Race and Unemployment: Labor Market Experiences of Black and White Men, 1968–1988," *Work and Occupations* 22, no. 3 (Aug. 1995): 245–70; Ahituv, Tienda, and Hotz, "Pathways from School to Work"; Moss and Tilly, "Why Opportunity Isn't Knocking."

CHAPTER 5: EVALUATING
MARKET EXPLANATIONS

1. Meyer, Hadja, and Levenson, *Unpublished Report for the Maryland Equal Opportunity Commission*, 2.

2. Ibid., 4.

3. Ibid., 46.

4. Ibid., 18.

5. Klinkner and Smith, *The Unsteady March*.

6. Ibid., 48.

7. Moss and Tilly, "Why Opportunity Isn't Knocking"; D'Amico and Maxwell, "The Continuing Significance of Race."

8. Holzer, "Black Employment Problems"; Philip Moss and Chris Tilly, "Soft Skills and Race: An Investigation of Black Men's Employment Problems," *Work and Occupations* 23, no. 3 (Aug. 1996): 252–76.

9. D'Souza, *The End of Racism*.

10. Moss and Tilly, "Skills and Race in Hiring."

11. Joleen Kirshenman and Kathryn Neckerman, " 'We'd love to hire them but . . . ': The Meaning of Race for Employers," in *The Urban Underclass*, ed. Christopher Jencks and Paul E. Peterson (Washington D.C.: Brookings Institute, 1991).

12. Christopher Jencks, Lauri Perman, and Lee Rainwater, "What is a Good Job? A New Measure of Labor-Market Success," *American Journal of Sociology* 93, no. 6 (May 1988): 1322–57.

CHAPTER 6: EMBEDDED TRANSITIONS

1. Granovetter, "Economic Action and Social Structure."

CHAPTER 7: NETWORKS OF INCLUSION,
NETWORKS OF EXCLUSION

1. Lawrence Bobo and James R. Kluegel, "Opposition to Race Targeting," *American Sociological Review* 58 (1993): 443–64; Charlotte Steeh and Maria Krysan, "The Polls — Trends: Affirmative Action and the Public, 1970–1995," *Public Opinion Quarterly* 60 (1996): 128–58.

2. Portes, *The Economic Sociology of Immigration*.

3. W. Norton Grubb, *Learning to Work: The Case for Reintegrating Job Training and Education* (New York: Russell Sage Foundation, 1996).

4. Walter Powell and Laurel Smith-Doerr, "Networks in Economic Life," in *Handbook of Economic Sociology*, ed. Neil Smelser and Richard Swedberg (Princeton, N.J.: Princeton University Press, 1994), 374.

5. Ibid., 368–69.

CHAPTER 8: WHITE PRIVILEGE
AND BLACK ACCOMMODATION

1. Freeman and Holzer, *The Black Youth Employment Crisis;* Wilson, *The Truly Disadvantaged;* Paul Osterman, *Getting Started: The Youth Labor Market* (Cambridge: Massachusetts Institute of Technology Press, 1980).

2. John S. Butler and Charles C. Moskos, "Labor Force Trends: The Military as Data," in *America Becoming: Racial Trends and Their Consequences*, vol. 2, ed. Neil Smelser, William Julius Wilson, and Faith Mitchell (Washington, D.C.: National Academy Press, 2001).

3. Stephen Steinberg, *Turning Back: The Retreat from Racial Justice in American Thought and Policy* (Boston: Beacon Press, 1995); Jill Quadagno, *The Color of Welfare: How Racism Undermined the War on Poverty* (New York: Oxford University Press, 1994).

BIBLIOGRAPHY

Ahituv, Avner, Marta Tienda, and V. Joseph Hotz. 1997. "Pathways from School to Work Among Black, Hispanic, and White Young Men in the 1980s." Unpublished manuscript.

Allen, Walter, and Reynolds Farley. 1987. *The Color Line and the Quality of Life in America*. New York: Russell Sage Foundation.

Anderson, C. Arnold. 1994. *Black Labor, White Wealth: The Search for Power and Economic Justice*. Edgewood, Md.: Duncan and Duncan.

Anderson, Elijah. 1978. *A Place on the Corner*. Chicago: University of Chicago Press.

Arum, Richard, and Michael Hout. 1998. "The Early Returns: The Transition from School to Work in the United States." In *From School to Work: A Comparative Study of Educational Qualifications and Occupational Destinations*, edited by Y. Shavit and W. Muller. London: Clarendon Press.

Auletta, Ken. 1982. *The Underclass*. New York: Vintage Books.

Bailey, Thomas. 1995. *Learning to Work: Employer Involvement in School-to-Work Transition Programs*. Washington, D.C.: Brookings Institution.

Bates, Timothy. 1995. "Rising Skills Levels and Declining Labor Force Status Among African American Males." *Journal of Negro Education* 64, no. 3 (summer): 373–83.

Bell, Derrick. 1992. *Faces at the Bottom of the Well*. New York: Basic Books.

Belous, Richard. 1989. *The Contingent Economy: The Growth of the Temporary, Part-time, and Subcontracted Workforce*. Washington D.C.: National Planning Association.

Bills, David, Lelia B. Helms, and Mustafa Ozcan. 1995. "The Impact of Student Employment on Teachers' Attitudes and Behaviors Toward Working Students." *Youth and Society* 27: 169–93

Bloom, Gordon, and Herbert R. Northrop. 1977. *Economics of Labor Relations*. Homewood, Ill.: Richard D. Irwin.

Bobo, Lawrence, and Vincent L. Hutchings. 1996. "Perceptions of Racial Group Competition: Extending Blumer's Theory of Group Position to a Multiracial Social Context." *American Sociological Review* 61, no. 6 (Dec.): 951–72.

Bobo, Lawrence, and James R. Kluegel. 1993. "Opposition to Race Targeting." *American Sociological Review* 58: 443–64.

Bonacich, Edna. 1972. "A Theory of Ethnic Antagonism: The Split Labor Market." *American Sociological Review* 37: 547–59.

———. 1975. "Advanced Capitalism and Black/White Relations in the United States: A Split Labor Market Analysis." *American Sociological Review* 41: 34–51.

Bonilla-Silva, Eduardo. 1997. "Rethinking Racism: Toward a Structural Interpretation." *American Sociological Review* 62, no. 3 (June): 465–80.

Bound, John, and Richard Freeman. 1992. "What Went Wrong? The Erosion of Relative Earnings and Employment Among Young Black Men in the 1980s." *Quarterly Journal of Economics* 107, no. 1 (Feb.): 201–32.

Bound, John, and Harry J. Holzer. 1993. "Industrial Shifts, Skill Levels, and the Labor Market for Black and White Males." *Review of Economics and Statistics* 75, no. 3 (Aug.): 387–96.

Bourdieu, Pierre, and Loic Wacquant. 1992. *Invitation to Reflexive Sociology*. Chicago: University of Chicago Press.

Bourgois, Phillippe. 1995. *In Search Of Respect: Selling Crack in El Barrio*. Cambridge: Cambridge University Press.

Braddock, Jomills, and James McPartland. 1986. "Applicant Race and Job Placement Decisions: A National Survey Experiment," *International Journal of Sociology and Social Policy* 6: 3–24.

———. 1987. "How Minorities Continue to Be Excluded from Equal Employment Opportunities: Research on Labor Market and Institutional Barriers." *Journal of Social Issues* 43, no. 1: 5–39.

Briggs, Vernon, and Thomas Marshall. 1965. *The Negro in Apprenticeship.* New York: JAI Press.

Brinton, Mary, and Takehiko Kariya. 1998. "Institutional Embeddedness in Japanese Labor Markets." In *The New Institutionalism in Sociology,* edited by Mary Brinton and Victor Nee. New York: Russell Sage Foundation.

Butler, John S., and Charles C. Moskos. 2001. "Labor Force Trends: The Military as Data." In *America Becoming: Racial Trends and Their Consequences,* vol. 2, edited by Neil Smelser, William J. Wilson, and Faith Mitchell. Washington, D.C.: National Academy Press.

Cancio, Silvia A., David T. Evans, and David Maume. 1996. "Reconsidering the Declining Significance of Race: Racial Differences in Early Career Wages." *American Sociological Review* 61, no. 4 (Aug.): 541–56.

Carr, Rhoda V., James D. Wright, and Charles J. Brody. 1996. "Effects of High School Work Experience a Decade Later: Evidence from the National Longitudinal Survey." *Sociology of Education* 69, no. 1: 66–81.

Chaplin, Duncan, and Jane Hannaway. 1997. "High School Employment: Meaningful Connections for At-Risk Youth." Washington, D.C.: Urban Institute.

Cohn, Samuel, and Mark A. Fossett. 1995. "Why Racial Employment Inequality Is Greater in Northern Labor Markets: Regional Differences in White-Black Employment Differentials." *Social Forces* 74, no. 2 (Dec.): 511–42.

Coleman, James S. 1974. *Youth Transition to Adulthood.* Chicago: University of Chicago Press.

———. 1984. "The Transition from School to Work." *Research in Stratification and Mobility* 3: 27–59.

———. 1988. "Social Capital in the Creation of Human Capital" *American Journal of Sociology* 84: s95-s120.

Collins-Lowry, Sharon M. 1997. *Black Corporate Executives: The Making and Breaking of the Black Middle Class.* Philadelphia, Penn.: Temple University Press.

Committee for Economic Development. 1985. *Investing in Our Children: Business in the Public Schools.* New York: Committee for Economic Development.

Cross, Malcolm, and Douglas I. Smith. 1987. *Black Youth Futures, Ethnic Minorities and the Youth Training Scheme.* Leicester: National Youth Bureau.

D'Amico, Robert, and Nan L. Maxwell. 1994. "The Impact of Post-School Joblessness on Male Black-White Wage Differentials." *Industrial Relations* 33, no. 2: 184–205.

———. 1995. "The Continuing Significance of Race in Minority Male Jobless-ness." *Social Forces* 73, no. 3 (March): 969–91.

Darrity, William, J. Richard Dietrich, and David Guilkey. 1997. "African American Economic Gains: A Long-Term Assessment: Racial and Ethnic Inequality in the United States: A Secular Perspective." *Proceedings of the American Economic Association* 87, no. 2 (May): 301–305.

Davis, Angela. 1997. "Race and Criminalization: Black Americans and the Punishment Industry." In *The House that Race Built*, edited by Wahneema Lubiano. New York: Pantheon Books.

Desaran, Forrest, and Diane Keithly. 1994. "Teenagers in the U.S. Labor Force: Local Labor Markets, Race and Family." *Rural Sociology* 59, no. 4: 668–92.

D'Souza, Dinesh. 1995. *The End of Racism: Principles for a Multiracial Society.* New York: Free Press.

Duster, Troy. 1995. "Postindustrialization and Youth Unemployment: African Americans as Harbingers." In *Poverty, Inequality and the Future of Social Policy: Western States in the New World Order*, edited by Katherine McFate, Roger Lawson, and William J. Wilson. New York: Russell Sage Foundation.

Epstein, Joyce. 1990. "School and Family Connections: Theory, Research and Implications for Integrating Sociologies of Education and Family." In *Families in Community Settings: Interdisciplinary Perspectives*, edited by Donald Unger and Marvin B. Sussman. Binghamton, N.Y.: Haworth Press.

Farkas, George, and Kevin Vicknair. 1996. "Comment: The Need to Control for Cognitive Skill." *American Sociological Review* 61: 557–64.

Fix, Michael, and Raymond J. Struyk, eds. 1993. *Clear and Convincing Evidence: Measurement of Discrimination in America.* Washington, D.C.: Urban Institute.

Folbre, Nancy. 1999. *The New Field Guide to the U.S. Economy.* New York: New Press.

Frank, Kenneth A., and Jeffrey Y. Yasumoto. 1998. "Linking Action to Social Structure Within a System: Social Capital Within and Between Subgroups." *American Journal of Sociology* 104, no. 3 (Nov.): 642–86.

Freeman, Richard, and Harry J. Holzer. 1986. *The Black Youth Employment Crisis.* Chicago, Ill.: University of Chicago Press.

Freeman, Richard, and David A. Wise, eds. 1982. *The Youth Labor Market Problem: Its Nature, Causes, and Consequences.* Chicago: University of Chicago Press.

From School to Work. 1990. Princeton, N.J.: Policy Information Center, Educational Testing Service.

Gibbs, Jewell. 1988. *Young, Black and Male in America: An Endangered Species*. New York: Auburn House.

Glasgow, Douglas. 1980. *The Black Underclass: Poverty, Unemployment and Entrapment of Ghetto Youth*. New York: Vintage Books.

Gordon, David., Richard Edwards, and Michael Reich. 1982. *Segmented Work, Divided Workers*. Cambridge: Cambridge University Press.

Gordon. Milton. 1964. *Assimilation in American Life*. New York: Oxford University Press.

Granovetter, Mark. 1974. *Getting a Job: A Study of Contacts and Careers*. Cambridge, Mass.: Harvard University Press.

———. 1982. "The Strength of Weak Ties: A Network Theory Revisited." In *Social Structure and Network Analysis*, edited by Peter Marsden and Nan Lin. Beverly Hills, Ca.: Sage Publications.

———. 1985. "Economic Action and Social Structure: The Problem of Embeddedness." *American Journal of Sociology* 91: 481–510.

Granovetter, Mark, and Chris Tilly. 1988. "Inequality and Labor Processes." In *The Handbook of Sociology*, edited by Neil Smelser. Newbury Park, Ca.: Sage Publications.

Grant, David M. "African American Labor Market Incorporation in a Global City (California)." University of California at Los Angeles, 1998.

Greico, Margaret. 1987. *Keeping It in the Family: Social Networks and Employment Chance*. London: Tavistock Publications.

Grubb, W. Norton. 1996. *Learning to Work: The Case for Reintegrating Job Training and Education*. New York: Russell Sage Foundation.

Grubb, W. Norton, and Lorraine M. McDonnell. 1991. *Local Systems of Vocational Education and Job Training: Diversity, Interdependence, and Effectiveness*. Berkeley, Ca.: National Center for Research in Vocational Education.

Hamilton, Steven. 1987. "Apprenticeship as a Transition to Adulthood in West Germany." *American Journal of Education* 95, no. 2 (Feb.): 314–45.

———. 1987. "Work and Maturity: Occupational Socialization of Non-College Youth in the United States and West Germany." *Research in the Sociology of Education and Socialization* 7: 283–312.

Hammer, Torild. 1996. "Consequences of Unemployment in the Transition from Youth to Adulthood in a Life Course Perspective." *Youth and Society* 27, no. 4: 450–68.

Holzer, Harry J. 1986. "Informal Job Search and Black Youth Unemployment," National Bureau of Economic Research Working Paper 1860. Cambridge, Mass.: National Bureau of Economic Research.

———. 1994. "Black Employment Problems: New Evidence, Old Questions." *Journal of Policy Analysis and Management* 13, no. 4: 699–722.

———. 1996. *What Employers Want: Job Prospects for Less-Educated Workers.* New York: Russell Sage Foundation.

Horton, Haywood, Beverlyn Lundy, Cedric Herring, and Melvin E. Thomas. 2000. "Lost in the Storm: The Sociology of the Black Working Class, 1850 to 1990." *American Sociological Review* 65, no. 1: 128–37.

Hotz, V. Joseph, and Marta Tienda. 1998. "Education and Employment in a Diverse Society: Generating Inequality through the School-to-Work Transition." In *American Diversity: A Demographic Challenge for the Twenty-First Century,* edited by Nancy Denton and Stewart Tolnay. Albany: State University of New York Press.

Howe, Harold et al. 1988. *The Forgotten Half: Non-College Youth in America.* New York: William T. Grant Foundation Commission on Work, Family and Citizenship.

Jacobson, Matthew F. 1998. *Whiteness of a Different Color: European Immigrants and the Alchemy of Race.* Cambridge, Mass.: Harvard University Press.

Jencks, Christopher. 1972. *Inequality: A Reassessment of the Effect of Family and Schooling in America.* New York: Harper and Row.

Jencks, Christopher, Lauri Perman, and Lee Rainwater. 1988. "What is a Good Job? A New Measure of Labor-Market Success." *American Journal of Sociology* 93, no. 6 (May): 1322–57.

Jones, Jacqueline. 1998. *American Work: Four Centuries of Black and White Labor.* New York: W. W. Norton.

Kantor, Harvey. 1994. "Managing the Transition from School to Work: The False Promise of Youth Apprenticeship." *Teachers College Record* 95, no. 4 (summer): 442–61.

Kantor, Harvey, and David Tyack, eds. 1985. *Work, Youth, and Schooling: Historical Perspectives on Vocationalism in American Education.* Stanford, Ca.: Stanford University Press.

Kimmel, Michael. 1987. *Changing Men: New Directions in Research on Men and Masculinity.* Newbury Park, Ca.: Sage.

Kinder, Donald R., and Lynn M. Sanders. 1996. *Divided by Color: Racial Politics and Democratic Ideals.* Chicago: University of Chicago Press.

Kirschenman, Joleen, and Kathryn Neckerman. 1991. "'We'd love to hire them but . . .': The Meaning of Race for Employers." In *The Urban Underclass,* edited by Christopher Jencks and Paul Peterson. Washington, D.C.: Brookings Institution.

Klerman, Jacob A., and Lynn A. Karoly. 1994. "Young Men and the Transition to Stable Employment." *Monthly Labor Review* 117, no. 8 (August): 31–46.

Klinkner, Philip A., and Rogers M. Smith. 1999. *The Unsteady March: The Rise and Decline of Racial Inequality in America.* Chicago: University of Chicago Press.

Lerman, Robert I. 1996. *Helping Disconnected Youth by Improving Linkages Between High Schools and Careers.* Washington, D.C.: Urban Institute.

Lieberson, Stanley. 1980. *A Piece of the Pie: Blacks and White Immigrants Since 1880.* Berkeley, Ca.: University of California Press.

Liebow, Eliot. 1967. *Tally's Corner: A Study of Negro Streetcorner Men.* Boston: Little, Brown.

MacLeod, Jay. 1987. *Ain't No Makin' It: Leveled Aspirations in a Low Income Neighborhood.* Boulder, Colo.: Westview Press.

Mare, Robert. 1995. "Changes in Educational Attainment and School Enrollment." In *State of the Union,* edited by Reynolds Farley. New York: Russell Sage Foundation.

Massey, Douglas, and Nancy Denton. 1993. *American Apartheid: Segregation and the Making of the Underclass.* Cambridge, Mass.: Harvard University Press.

Mead, Lawrence. 1992. *The New Politics of Poverty.* New York: Basic Books.

Meyer, Edmund, Yvonne Hajda, and Bernard Levenson. 1969. *Unpublished Report for the Maryland Equal Opportunity Commission Supervised by James Coleman, Johns Hopkins University Center for the Social Organization of Schools.* Baltimore: Maryland Equal Opportunity Commission.

Moss, Philip, and Chris Tilly. 1991. "Why Opportunity Isn't Knocking: Racial Inequality and the Demand for Labor." In *Urban Inequality: Evidence From Four Cities,* edited by Alicia O'Connor, Chris Tilly, and Lawrence Bobo. New York: Russell Sage.

———. 1995. "Skills and Race in Hiring: Quantitative Findings from Face to Face Interviews." *Eastern Economic Journal* 21, no. 3: 357–74.

———. 1996. "Soft Skills and Race: An Investigation of Black Men's Employment Problems." *Work and Occupations* 23, no. 3 (Aug.): 252–76.

Muller, Walter, and Yossi Shavit. 1998. "The Institutional Embeddedness of the Stratification Process: A Comparative Study of Qualifications and Occupations in Thirteen Countries." In *From School to Work: A Comparative Study of Educational Qualifications and Occupational Destinations,* edited by Yossi Shavit and Walter Muller. London: Clarendon Press.

Murray, Charles. 1984. *Losing Ground: American Social Policy 1950–1980.* New York: Basic Books.

Neale, Derek, and William Johnson. 1996. "The Role of Premarket Factors in Black-White Wage Differences." *Journal of Political Economy* 104, no. 5: 869–95.

Neckerman, Kathryn, and Joleen Kirschenman. 1991. "Hiring Strategies, Racial Bias, and Inner-City Workers: An Investigation of Employers' Hiring Decisions." *Social Problems* 38: 433–47.

Nee, Victor. 1998. "Embeddedness and Beyond: Institutions, Exchange and Social Structure." In *The New Institutionalism in Sociology*, edited by Mary Brinton and Victor Nee. New York: Russell Sage Foundation.

Oakes, Jeannie. 1985. *Keeping Track: How Schools Structure Inequality*. New Haven, Conn.: Yale University Press.

Oliver, Melvin, and Thomas Shapiro. 1997. *Black Wealth, White Wealth: A New Perspective on Racial Inequality*. New York: Routledge Press.

Osterman, Paul. 1980. *Getting Started: The Youth Labor Market*. Cambridge, Mass.: Massachusetts Institute of Technology Press.

———. 1995. "Is There a Problem with the Youth Labor Market, and If So, How Should We Fix It?" In *Poverty, Inequality and the Future of Social Policy: Western States and the New World Order*, edited by Katherine McFate, Roger Lawson, and William J. Wilson. New York: Russell Sage Foundation.

Parnes, Herbert, and Andrew I. Kohen. 1975. "Occupational Information and Labor Market Status: The Case of Young Men," *Journal of Human Resources* 10, no. 1: 44–55.

Peterson, George E., and Wayne Vroman. 1992. *Urban Labor Markets and Job Opportunities*. Washington, D.C.: Urban Institute.

Petterson, Stephen M. 1997. "Are Young Black Men Really Less Willing to Work?" *American Sociological Review* 62 (Aug.): 605–13.

Portes, Alejandro. 1994. *The Economic Sociology of Immigration: Essays on Networks, Ethnicity and Entrepreneurship*. New York: Russell Sage Press.

Portes, Alejandro, and Patricia Landolt. 1996. "Unsolved Mysteries: The Downside of Social Capital." *American Prospect* 7, no. 26: 28–31.

Portes, Alejandro, and Julia S. Sensenbrenner. 1993. "Embeddedness and Immigration: Notes on the Social Determination of Embeddedness." *American Journal of Sociology* 98, no. 6: 1320–51.

Powell, Walter, and Laurel Smith-Doerr. 1994. "Networks in Economic Life." In *Handbook of Economic Sociology*, edited by Neil Smelser and Richard Swedberg. Princeton, N.J.: Princeton University Press.

Quadagno, Jill. 1994. *The Color of Welfare: How Racism Undermined the War on Poverty*. New York: Oxford University Press.

Reskin, Barbara F., and Heidi Hartman. 1986. *Women's Work, Men's Work: Sex Segregation on the Job.* Washington, D.C.: National Academy Press.

Roediger, David. 1991. *The Wages of Whiteness: Race and the Making of the American Working Class.* London: Verso.

Rosenbaum, James E. 1996. "Policy Uses of Research on the High School-to-Work Transition." *Sociology of Education* 69 (extra issue): 102–22.

Rosenbaum, James E., and Takehiko Kariya. 1989. "From High School to Work: Market and Institutional Mechanisms in Japan." *American Journal of Sociology* 94, no. 6: 1334–65.

Rosenbaum, James E., Takehiko Kariya, Rick Setterstein, and Tony Maier. 1990. "Market and Network Theories of the Transition from High School to Work: Their Application to Industrialized Societies." *Annual Review of Sociology* 16: 263–99.

Rubin, Lillian. 1994. *Families on the Faultline: America's Working Class Speaks About the Family, the Economy, Race and Ethnicity.* New York: Harper Collins.

Ruhm, Christopher. 1997. "Is High School Employment Consumption or Investment?" Washington, D.C.: Employment Policies Institute.

Sennet, Richard, and Jonathan Cobb. 1972. *The Hidden Injuries of Class.* New York: Knopf.

Steeh, Charlotte, and Maria Krysan. 1996. "The Polls — Trends: Affirmative Action and the Public, 1970–1995." *Public Opinion Quarterly* 60: 128–58

Steinberg, Stephen. 1989. *The Ethnic Myth: Race, Ethnicity, and Class in America.* Boston: Beacon Press.

———. 1995. *Turning Back: The Retreat from Racial Justice in American Thought and Policy.* Boston: Beacon Press.

Stewart, James B. 1997. "Recent Perspectives on African-Americans in Post-Industrial Labor Markets." *American Economic Review* 87, no. 2: 315–21.

Sullivan, Mercer. 1989. *"Getting Paid": Youth, Crime and Work in the Inner City.* Ithaca, N.Y.: Cornell University Press.

Sum, Andrew, N. Fogg, and Robert Taggart. 1988. *Withered Dreams: The Decline in the Economic Fortunes of Young, Non-College Educated Male Adults and Their Families.* New York: William T. Grant Commission on Family, Work, and Citizenship.

Taylor, Marylee. 1995. "White Backlash to Workplace Affirmative Action: Peril or Myth?" *Social Forces* 73: 1385–1414.

Tiemeyer, Peter. 1990. "Racial Differences in the Transition to Stable Employment for Young Males." Paper presented at the American Sociological Association meeting, Washington, D.C., August 1990.

Tienda, Marta, and V. Joseph Hotz. 1990. *Pathways from School to Work: Discontinuities in the School-Work Transition of Minority Youth*. New York: Russell Sage Foundation.

Tienda, Marta, and Haya Stier. 1996. "Generating Labor Market Inequality: Employment Opportunities and Accumulation of Disadvantage." *Social Problems* 43, no. 2 (May): 147–65.

Tilly, Chris. 1998. *Durable Inequality*. Berkeley: University of California Press.

Tomaskovic-Devey, Donald. 1993. *Gender and Racial Inequality at Work*. Ithaca, N.Y.: ILR Press.

Tonry, Michael H. 1995. *Malign Neglect: Race, Crime and Punishment in America*. New York: Oxford University Press.

Tuch, Stephen A., and Jack K. Martin, eds. 1997. *Racial Attitudes in the 1990's: Continuity and Change*. Westport, Conn.: Praeger.

Turner, Margery A., Michael Fix, and Raymond J. Struyk. 1991. *Opportunities Denied, Opportunities Diminished: Racial Discrimination in Hiring*. Washington D.C.: Urban Institute Press.

U.S. Bureau of the Census. *County Business Patterns, Maryland*. Washington, D.C.: U.S. Government Printing Office.

———. *County and City Data Book*. Washington, D.C.: U.S. Government Printing Office.

———. *Statistical Abstracts of the U.S. National Data Book*. Washington, D.C.: U.S. Government Printing Office.

U.S. Department of Labor. *Report on the American Workforce*. Washington, D.C.: U.S. Government Printing Office.

———. *Occupational Handbook*. Washington, D.C.: U.S. Government Printing Office.

Veum, Jonathan R. 1993. "Training Among Young Adults: Who, What Kind, and for How Long?" *Monthly Labor Review* 116, no. 8 (Aug.): 27–32.

Veum, Jonathan R., and A. B. Weiss. 1993. "Education and the Work Histories of Young Adults." *Monthly Labor Review* 116, no. 4 (Apr.): 11–20.

Wacquant, Loic. 1989. "The Ghetto, the State, and the New Capitalist Economy." *Dissent* 36, no. 4: 508–20.

Waldinger, Roger. 1995. "The 'Other Side' of Embeddedness: A Case Study of the Interplay of Economy and Ethnicity." *Ethnic and Racial Studies* 18, no. 3: 555–80.

———. 1996. *Still the Promised City: African American and New Immigrants in New York*. Cambridge, Mass.: Harvard University Press.

Waldinger, Roger, and Thomas Bailey. 1991. "The Continuing Significance of

Race: Racial Conflict and Racial Discrimination in Construction." *Politics and Society* 19, no. 3: 291–323.

Weiss, Lois, and Michelle Fine. 1988. *The Unknown City*. Boston: Beacon Press.

Wellman, David. 1997. "Angry White Men." In *Racial Attitudes in the 1990s: Continuity and Change*, edited by Steven A. Tuch and Jack K. Martin. Westport, Conn.: Praeger.

Williams, Donald. 1987. *Labor Force Participation of Black and White Youth*. Ann Arbor: University of Michigan Press.

Wilson, Franklin D., Marta Tienda, and Lawrence Wu. 1995. "Race and Unemployment: Labor Market Experiences of Black and White Men, 1968–1988." *Work and Occupations* 22, no. 3 (Aug.): 245–70.

Wilson, George. 1997. "Pathways to Power: Racial Differences in the Determinants of Job Authority." *Social Problems* 44 (Feb.): n.p.

Wilson, William J. 1980. *The Declining Significance of Race*, 2d ed. Chicago: University of Chicago Press.

———. 1987. *The Truly Disadvantaged: The Inner City, the Underclass and Public Policy*. Chicago: University of Chicago Press.

———. 1996. *When Work Disappears: The World of the New Urban Poor*. New York: Knopf.

Wolkinson, Benjamin. 1973. *Blacks, Unions, and the EEOC: A Study of Administrative Failure*. Lexington, Mass.: Lexington Books.

INDEX

Compositor:	BookMatters
Text:	10/15 Janson
Display:	Janson
Printer and Binder:	Maple-Vail Manufacturing Group